# THE

# BLACK LIST

## 1526 - 2022

AN ABRIDGED HISTORY OF STRUCTURAL RACISM IN
AMERICA

**MARQUIS D. BYNUM**

# ABOUT THE AUTHOR

**Marquis D. Bynum** is the curator of the @Black_Ourstory Instagram page and author of the best-selling e-book "The List: From Slavery to George Floyd," which reached more than 700,000 readers and is currently implemented in history, race, and culture studies worldwide.

He is a 2008 graduate of DePauw University and earned a master's degree in 2011 from Indiana State University. Marquis currently serves as an all-source intelligence analyst in the United States Air Force and a strategic military analyst studying Latin American and Caribbean affairs for the United States Army. After three military deployments and more than 12 years of studying the Middle East, Africa, and Latin America, "The Black List: 1526-2022" is his personal ode to American history.

He enjoys spending time with his wife and two dogs and giving back to the San Antonio, Texas, community as the co-founder of Project H.E.L.P. (Humanity Evolves from Loving People), a non-profit organization dedicated to inspiring communities to provide charitable solutions for the houseless and less fortunate and providing educational mentorship opportunities for children and teens living in underserved communities.

# THE
# BLACK LIST
## 1526 - 2022

Bird House Publishing
8325 Broadway Street, Pearland, TX 77581
(832) 535-2362

Bird House Publishing is committed to filling the need
for more diverse books. We are also committed to the
relentless pursuit of equity, authenticity, and inclusion.
We encourage all of our readers and authors to show
up in the world as their best selves. All of our works
are curated to build empathy, coping skills, courage,
and curiosity. We are always looking for diverse and
thoughtful voices to share with the world.

Bird House Publishing rev date 05/27/22

To my family, kinfolk, and especially to
Emma Louise House,

For always telling me,

"We must do what we have to do in
order to do what we want to do."

# THE BLACK LIST
# 1526 - 2022

496 years. 100 historical facts. This book is a brief museum of Black exploration that connects the very first Angolans enslaved in America and the post-Civil War illusions of freedom to the Civil Rights struggles of the 1950s and 60s, the War on Drugs, all the way to the Obama, Trump, and Biden Administrations. All of this while capturing the history before and after the Civil Rights Summer of 2020 following the deaths of Ahmaud Arbery, Breonna Taylor, George Floyd, and countless others.

Because contrary to popular belief, history does not exist in a vacuum.

Racism and discrimination no longer need their signature white hoods, water hoses, bombings, and "White's only" signs. Although still very much present, they have learned to disguise themselves quite cleverly. A chameleon of sorts, bigotry has seamlessly shifted its colors among false political promises, hyperbolic media opinion, cultural misinterpretations, irrelevant distractions, and the sensationalized noise of too many who believe financial success equates to racial invincibility—or invisibility.

*"Kuz even if you in a Benz..."*

Meanwhile, our history is on the verge of extinction and fighting on contested grounds for its survival, waging war between its truth being exposed for the sake of societal progress or finding itself silenced and replaced by a fantasy of denial and colorblind debate.

History is all we have to learn the truth about ourselves. History is also all we have to ensure some actual progress is made and generational mistakes are no longer repeated. History is a lot closer than we think and...

**Everything Is Connected.**

# CONTENT &
# TIMELINE

# THE INTRO:

## POEMS, PROTESTS &
## ORIGINS OF THE BLACK LIST

August 26, 2016. Inside Levi's Stadium. Hundreds
made the drive to Santa Clara, California, to celebrate
the opening of another NFL season. Fans adorned in
red and gold littered the parking lot to enjoy the
tailgating festivities while others made their way
through the maze of corridors, ramps, stairs, and
spontaneously choreographed war chants -

"LET'S GO, NI-NERS!"

The San Francisco 49ers were hosting the Green Bay
Packers, and although the stadium wasn't packed, the
crowd exuded the same energy as if it were a sold-out
playoff game. And it made sense. This was a team just
three years removed from a Super Bowl trip where
they would lose to the Baltimore Ravens in that weird
lights out game and where a second-year backup
named Colin Kaepernick would make his grand debut

But this game, three years later, would be very different.

The Packers jogged onto the field first. The players finished their last bit of stretching and route running before the official game time whistle blew. Soon after, the stadium announcer asked those in attendance to stand and get ready for the home team. The sprinkling of fans scattered throughout a sea of empty seats orated their arrival with boisterous cheers. As the flames flamed and the stadium speakers boomed with some heavy rock song from the 1980s, the 49ers ran out onto the field to the music of their audience, heading straight to the end zone to take a quick knee in prayer.

It was game day.

As the players wrapped up their "Amens," stadium staff wheeled out a mobile stage into the end zone where local opera singer Chris Pucci was awaiting at a microphone. Two military service members were standing behind him. One held the California flag, while the other held "Old Glory" – the American flag. Then, the announcer came back on, asking the fans to remain standing and remove their hats in preparation for the Star-Spangled Banner. As Mr. Pucci opened his rendition with a strong vibrato, rockets boomed in the speakers for extra effect, and the crowd roared over the opera. And while everyone listened, sang, screamed, and waved in their own star-spangled way, two players on the San Francisco sideline were sitting on the bench.

This was a protest. And it wasn't the first time.

Two preseason games prior, 49ers safety Eric Reid and quarterback Colin Kaepernick had sat on the bench during the anthem. Kaepernick wasn't dressed to play, so maybe no one took notice, but in this third game, the red number 7 with the afro picked out was hard to miss. The next morning, a California-sized wild fire rapidly spread through the country. Everywhere you looked, you couldn't help but see it. Even if you weren't a fan and couldn't care less about football, you had an opinion about it. It was easily one of the most controversial moments in recent memory. No one even cared about the outcome of the game — the Niners lost 10-21 — nor did they care that the team went 2 and 14 that season.

The only point of concern for anyone was for the man who had just volunteered himself to become the new face of protests against police brutality and violence and the metaphor of what it meant to live in "2 Americas."

I didn't know it at the time, but it was in that moment that "The Black List" began to take shape. I found myself investing way too much time in the narratives of those on Fox News, the debates on CNN, and the opinions of the greatest minds on Earth – the Facebook comment section. I became frustrated in their conscious effort to divert from what Kaepernick had addressed very pointedly in his post-game interview:

*"I am not going to stand up to show pride in a flag*
*for a country that oppresses Black people and people*
*of color. To me, this is bigger than football, and it*
*would be selfish on my part to look the other way.*
*There are bodies in the street and people getting*
*paid leave and getting away with murder."*

How easily they shifted those words into one of being
"disrespectful" to the military and some egregious
affront to the memories of those long past and
especially those who made the Ultimate Sacrifice.
There were athletes left and right digging in their
family archives to find a relative who had served.
Those against him were using the memoirs to say he
offended their granddad. Those for him used theirs to
say the ancestral soldiers fought for his right to protest.
Everyone used everyone to squeeze in their opinion.
Never mind the fact that Nate Boyer, a U.S. Army
Green Beret, held a conversation with Kaepernick and
told him about the significance of kneeling at military
funerals to honor the fallen, which was incorporated
into the quarterback's pregame ritual rather than sitting
on the bench. Never mind the fact that the Department
of Defense paid almost seven million dollars to sports
teams to hold the National Anthem before every game
as a means of military recruitment. And especially
never mind the very bold fact of what that bent knee
meant in the first place — the disproportionate killing of
Black and Brown men and women by police officers
and the consistency of "paid leave" and "not guilty"
verdicts.

His opponents continually detracted from the main point of his argument in favor of attaching his material and financial success. He had made it to the proverbial mountain top and accomplished the so-called "American Dream." What reason did he have to complain? To these people, somehow reaching a certain salary cap apparently shields one's experiences from racism and discrimination. But I also came to understand that, again, their arguments of monetary success were the primary determinate that our society was as far from the days of slavery and civil rights as we could be. "Hey, you guys can be millionaires now. Let it go." For them, Dr. King's "Dream" was, in fact, now a reality, as if the ability to obtain money was the only demand to represent Black equality and justice in America. Somehow. Someway. I knew I needed to disprove this theory.

At the time, I knew there were very historical reasons for the mistrust between police and Black folks in this country and the violence that followed. What I didn't know was the history and the details well enough to let them know. But I was determined to try to paint that picture. The conversation surrounding Colin Kaepernick's actions played out on every channel. And every Sunday, I watched the cameras from every game search around the field to see who was kneeling and who was standing.

It was as if the NFL and the television executives didn't even care about the game anymore. Just those first few moments before kickoff. That was the high drama, the ratings. If it kneels, it reels. It became clear to me that I needed to find a way to get people to understand what the hell was going on.

I realized a long time ago to quit debating with people genuinely not invested in learning or hearing an alternative side to their own beliefs and opinions. So, challenging one's feelings regarding the National Anthem or what America means to them would have been a terrible approach. It's far too subjective and America does not and cannot mean the same to everyone. So I knew I needed another angle.

History.

History is a field that cares nothing for your feelings or emotions. It just exists within itself as a factual point of events along a very long continuum of more factual events—all directly and indirectly connected to one another, no matter if anyone realizes it or not. For the most part, history in itself remains unchallengeable. Sure, we learn new things that change or expand our previous versions of historical fact. And absolutely sure, there are those who knowingly or unknowingly twist and turn the motivations behind actual events or tell half-truths, our favorite tactic. But with a little more non-confirmation-biased Google and book digging, the truth is always right there. Waiting to be discovered.

And this is where I began my journey.

I didn't start at the entrance of African and Black people in America because I still had no clue what I was getting into. So, I just began at the very center of the debate, the National Anthem itself. Like most Americans, I had been singing this song since childhood. Now I realize that was quite forcibly done and had a very nationalistic brainwashing scheme behind it. Nevertheless, it seemed harmless. I mean, every country has its song that exemplifies its nation's longevity, pride, and struggle, right? So why shouldn't we?

Hell, I even remember when my high school in San Antonio introduced the "Texas National Anthem," which, thank the Heavens, my mother told me I would sit down for. "You ain't pledging to no damn Texas! You will sit, do you hear me? I don't care if you the only one!" If you know my mom, you read that in her voice. Besides, I'm from Tampa, so pledging to "Texas, Our Texas" would have been traitorous. And in a bit of pre-Kaepernick fashion, I was the only one in my class who did sit, and I can assure you it felt awkward. But looking back, I'm glad my mother pushed that courage on me and the notion that I would never go along with anything simply because the majority did.

Because the loneliest of roads can be worth the drive sometimes.

So, the Star-Spangled Banner it was. Which is really a poem called "Defence of Fort M'Henry." I had to know what exactly made it so star-spangled and why he took a knee during that song.

I first had to study the man who penned it: Francis Scott Key, a famed lawyer, prison negotiator, and pro-slavery enslaver. Okay, strike one and two. I then learned that there were four stanzas to the song. We only sing the first one. But upon reading that third stanza, I almost took a knee at my own computer.

*"No refuge could save the hireling and slave / From the terror of flight or the gloom of the grave."*

Translation: Francis Scott Key casually jabs at the enslaved persons killed by the American colonists while attempting to hide or run away to freedom, all while "the bombs were bursting in air." Strike three. But understanding our nation's anthem and the pro-slavery stance of its author wasn't nearly enough to get them to understand the significance of the kneel. Going back and forth between the history books and the commentary surrounding the protests, I found myself frustrated again. The American hypocrisy on display was beyond annoying. This was the same country that had just mourned the death of Muhammad Ali two months prior in June, and now here we were in August, calling Colin Kaepernick a traitor.

And then it hit me. They only "loved" Ali after his Parkinson's silenced him. Never before. They erased that boisterous, confident Black man who joined the Nation of Islam at that time in history and sacrificed everything to defy the government's orders not to go to war with Vietnam because his war was with America. Instead, they inserted their fleeting adoration for the meek and trembling shadow of the former champ.

Oh, how we love remembering the sides of people we prefer and not the totality of their being.

This task surely was going to require a stiff drink and more research. Would the anthem defenders believe me if I said the song was only meant for White men and its author was a slave owner? Or would they do what they've always done—remind me that

"That was a long time ago. Things have changed now. The song is different now."

"America is different. We are in a post-racial society now. Hey, we had a Black president, remember?"

Oh, how we also love to rewrite history to fit our narratives.

I had to dig deeper and somehow connect our history, and not just Black history, but American history, to the kneeling in 2016. I had to make them see. I needed them to know the history, sure, but I really wanted them to see what Black people had gone through in this country and are still going through, in the hopes that could be enough to create some empathy and awareness which would shift minority and fringe narratives to the forefront and ultimately warrant a reassessment of the current lens of America.

I kept digging further and further, from learning about Francis Scott Key to understanding the War of 1812, the war about which the song was written. I then discovered the beef between the U.S. and the British. The American Revolution. The first English men and women who landed in Native American Virginia and the Spanish and Portuguese explorers who settled in St. Augustine, Florida and brought the first enslaved Africans to the New World in the early 1500s. I then bounced into really learning the traumas of slavery and the laws enacted to ensure generational dependence, poverty, enslavement, and illiteracy. I moved on past slavery to examine the 100-year Jim Crow, segregation and civil rights era which we often celebrate as if it's some Disney movie. The protagonist: Black People. The villain: The racist south. The climax of the movie: Martin Luther King's Dream in Washington. The happy ending: The Civil Rights Act of 1964 and 1965. Cue joyful song and roll credits. It's almost as if some congressional bills magically ended systemic racism and discrimination in the country and culminated into a joyous song like "A Whole New World." But our story is closer to The Princess and the Frog - "Almost There."

I literally had to unlearn and relearn everything. I kept jotting down dates, events, and people and over time, it grew into this museum of

Black History in the notes section of my iPhone. I was beginning to see the dots connect in this Russell Crowe "Beautiful Mind" type of way, but with more Black people. I felt selfish, and I wanted to get these stories out of my phone and into the world. Maybe others wanted to know things they were never told either.

So, on September 16, 2016 (almost a month from when Kaepernick and Reid sat on that bench), I posted a really rough version called "The List" on my Facebook. We all know nobody reads long posts on Facebook, but this one did well unexpectedly. Hundreds of likes and almost the same number of shares. That's when I knew that maybe I had something.

Four years later, I put that endeavor to the side to build my Black History page on Instagram (@Black_Ourstory). By that, I mean talking to myself and the maybe 100 followers who were only following and hitting the like button purely out of sympathetic friendship duties (I love y'all for that). I had no real direction with that thing. I was just doing it because the great director/storyteller John Singleton had passed, and I wanted to help continue telling our stories as he did. Then the "Civil Rights Summer of 2020" began and changed everything.

Ahmaud Arbery shot down by two White men in February. Breonna Taylor shot and killed while sleeping in her apartment in March. And the 8 minutes and 46-second knee to the neck of George Floyd in May. It was incredibly overwhelming. Personally, I was distant. But, mentally, I was in one of the worst places I had ever been. My usual vices of poetry and bourbon carried me as I existed in a sort of ghostly paralysis, just languishing through the days and having a complete out-of-body experience.

Ahmaud Arbery's murder really shook me. The cop-on-Black killings happened so often that I had normalized and compartmentalized them in this vicarious PTSD corner of my brain to function throughout the days. But the fact that two regular, everyday citizens — a father and son assassination crew and another man who filmed the entire murder — could drive up to someone, demand answers about his whereabouts, kill him in the middle of the street in broad daylight and then just go back home, crack open a cold brew to celebrate, call the police and tell them what they had just done, and not be arrested or charged whatsoever. I mean, absolutely nothing happened to them until the video leaked a whole three months later and the police were then forced to do something.

I realized then that our deaths had to go viral just for us to be able to have a discussion about it. Not a warrant, subpoena, or conviction. Just a discussion. That cut deep.

I would be in my office late through the night, fighting back the tears. Sometimes I would let go and just lose that fight on purpose. I needed the cry. I just couldn't understand why they couldn't understand. How could Kaepernick's knee mean more to them than Derek Chauvin's? We were four years removed from Kaepernick and had accumulated four years' worth of more dead Black bodies, and they still didn't get it. It seemed that no one at work cared or attempted to care. The military was eerily too silent. We could discuss suicide and sexual assault but not the demise of Black lives. And those who weren't silent chose to relish in their own commentary on what Black people *should* do when approached by officers. "Maybe if he had just complied...." They became riot analysts, assessing the burnings of a Target and arguing what Martin Luther King Jr. would have and would not have agreed with. Some even had the audacity to tell Bernice King, daughter of the late reverend, what her father would have preferred.

No one was looking at the root causes. So, I decided I had to.

Completely unplanned, but just like in 2016, I was over and done with all the opinionated commentary. So I blew the dust off *The List*, cleaned up the history points, made a cool, bright, easy-to-read poster version, and attached a detailed PDF copy with 272 sources as backup. And on June 24, 2020, amid a global pandemic and a nationwide protest to protect Black and Brown lives, *The List: From Slavery to George Floyd* was published. This time around, the feedback was incredible, reaching close to a million people! Okay, like 700,000 something, but still.

Celebrities, athletes (thank you, Ray Allen), musicians and rappers (thank you, Chance the Rapper), actors and actresses, and even universities seeking a new summer lecture topic to discuss the current climate tensions all reached out. I finally felt like we could make some actual progress. And with history — Black history — leading the way.

In a weird way, I'm thankful for the summer of 2020. Amidst an immense depth of sadness and anger, I found my purpose and direction. And while it was a moment of genuine happiness for me, I knew that it would be that one thing I was hoping for that would help explain not only Kaepernick's protests but also the protests of 2020, 1965, 1865, and 1526. It was, maybe, that one thing they finally needed to see … even if they didn't want to.

And for one last time, I wanted to be sure the point was made clear.

*The Black List: 1526-2022.*

This is the third and final iteration of this literary body of work. All the labor that went into this took place over six years. I've learned so much more and I've realized just how much I missed in the previous versions. I've put everything I got into this one. And in full transparency, I am absolutely elated to be done with this thing. It has truly been one of the most daunting challenges of my life and, at the same time, the most fulfilling thing I've ever done. I legitimately have a new outlook on my own unique privilege of existing in this space, even amidst the present-day issues plaguing Black America, simply because I've grown to realize that where I am right now, today, in this place and time, was someone's wildest dreams 50, 70, 100, and 496 years ago.

That is something I treat with the utmost care. And at the same time, I remind myself to continue the labor to make sure this place is better for someone else 50, 70, 100, and 496 years from now because societal progress and the betterment of everyone are always worth it. It has to be.

I often say, "History does not exist in a vacuum. Everything is connected." And hopefully, I was able to convey that while paying proper homage and respect to those who had lost their lives, those who gave their lives, and those hoping to live their lives. I genuinely hope this serves as a guide to help you learn, unlearn, and relearn just who we've been, who we are, and who we have a chance to be, if only for the sake of our sanity and the security of our humanity.

**Forever Humbled and Thankful,**
**Marquis D. Bynum**

*"If a race has no history, if it has no worthwhile tradition, it becomes a negligible factor in the thought of the world, and it stands in the danger of being exterminated."*

*– Dr. Carter G. Woodson*

# AFRICAN

# CHAPTER I:
# 1526-1865

## The American African
## In a Brave New World

*"There is no [one] Garden of Eden in Africa. Or
if there is a Garden of Eden, it is Africa."*

*The Motherland. The 1st humans turned to tribes. Tribes
turned to communal villages. Villages expanded into cities.
Cities into kingdoms. And kingdoms into empires. Each
possessing its own unique culture, customs, and traditions.
One influencing the other in an interconnected universe of
Blackness. The continent that literally changed the world.
And in return, the world forever changed Africa.*

*From the early 1500s to 1903, eight to nine million Africans
were trafficked to the Middle East during the Arab Slave
Trade. It was the second-largest human trafficking event ever.
But the first? The European Transatlantic Slave Trade.*

*Between 1525 and 1860, Spanish, Portuguese, Dutch and English ships human trafficked 12.5 million Africans. Of that estimation, at least 10.7 million would survive the horrific 90-day journey across the Atlantic Ocean, otherwise known as the Middle Passage, only to arrive in the Americas, a strange New World.*

*While the vast majority of exhausted, confused, terrified, and barely living Africans were disembarked on the shores of South America and the Caribbean, 388,000 would find their lives forever changed and bound to a life of servitude and chattel slavery in the newly expanding colonies of America.*

**This is the Enslavement Era.**

## 1. 1526. The First 100.

The first **100 Africans** are trafficked from Angola, Africa, to the Spanish colony of San Miguel de Gualdape (present-day Winyah Bay, South Carolina) and governed by the wealthy Spanish explorer Lucas Vásquez de Ayllón. Due to the unfamiliarity with the land and a lack of survival knowledge, the colony faces starvation, sickness, and death. The Angolans take advantage of the situation, burn down the settlement, and are rumored to have escaped to nearby native villages. They are never heard from again. [1][2][3][4]

## 2. 1619. "20 and Odd Negroes."

**"About the latter end of August, a Dutch man of warr of the burden of a 160 tunes arrived at Point-Comfort... He brought not any thing but 20 and odd Negroes, which the Governor and Cape Merchant bought for victualls." - John Rolfe, August 1619.** Ninety-three years later, the next **20 Angola Africans** are stolen, purchased, and imported by the English, this time to the Powhatan Chiefdom known as Tsenacommacah. [5][6] *Which is Native American for "This was our land until the English invaded it, conquered it, and re-renamed it to Hampton, Virginia."* This tribe is the same Powhatan tribe of Amonute, who had just passed two years prior at the age of 21. *You know her by her nickname, Pocahontas, or her kidnapped, married, Christianized name, Rebecca Rolfe. Wife of John Rolfe, witness to the first 20 enslaved Africans.* [7] The human cargo that arrives in Virginia comes from the port city of Luanda,

THE BLACK LIST: 1526 - 2022

a Portuguese colony now and the capital of present-day Angola later. Most of the enslaved reaching the New World were captured during an ongoing war between Portugal and the Kingdom of Ndongo. **Queen Ann Nzingha**, aka "The Mother of Angola," will eventually lose this war, and the country will become a prime location for the **Transatlantic Slave Trade**. An estimated 50,000 enslaved persons brought to the Americas were from Angola. [89] *Because our history is based in England and not Spain or Portugal, the year 1619 is often erroneously referred to as the beginning of American enslavement. But to remedy this error,* **(See #1)** .

## 3. 1640-1641. The Legalization of Slavery.

Chattel slavery as an institution is not a thing yet. Instead, indentured servitude is the trending topic. *Chattel slavery meant that one person (the master) had total proprietary ownership of another (the enslaved), and the enslaved person was sub-human compared to a laborer or indentured servant.* Most workers in the New World are European and African indentured servants and a sprinkling of violently coerced Native Americans. That is until Virginia sentences indentured servant **John Punch** to 30 lashes and a lifetime of servitude for running away from a tobacco field. [10] Victor and James Gregory, the two European indentured servants Punch ran away with, also receive 30 lashes but only four years of additional servitude. The Virginia courts also punish John Punch's children with the same status as their father. *This is the first time in history that slavery has been codified and legalized as an institution, and legal differences between American African and American European – Black and White – are established.* One year later, Massachusetts becomes the first state to fully legalize slavery as an institution **(See #11)**. [11]

**4. 1655-1656.**

**Elizabeth Key**, born to an enslaved woman and a White Englishmen, sues for her freedom after being sold to two different owners. Under English Common Law, the father's status determined the status of a newborn child, and Englishmen could not keep baptized Christians enslaved. Elizabeth was a baptized member of the Church of England, and her father was European—two strikes under English law. One year later, after getting help to gather the necessary proof, she wins her freedom. [12] But her victory comes at a cost for everyone else enslaved after her, and the colonies waste no time amending their laws **(See #5)**.

**5. 1662-1680. The Slave Codes.**

Six years after Elizabeth Key wins her freedom, 22 years after John Punch **(See #3)** is sentenced and 203 years before the "Black Codes" are passed **(See #31)**, the colonies enact the first set of new laws for the enslaved. [13] The colonial governments invent the Slave Codes to reduce American European paranoia about rebellion and escape and keep their free labor intact. Thanks to the victory of Elizabeth Key, Virginia passes the first code - **the Hereditary Slave Law** - and children will now have the same status as their mothers **(See #4)**. [14] *Now slavery has become generational, and White owners/fathers are not legally responsible for*

*children with enslaved women.* Other Slave Codes passed:
1667. Christianity and baptism did not make you free,
another Elizabeth Key effect **(See #4 Again)**. 1672. Any
White man who wounded or killed a runaway enslaved
person would not be prosecuted, just ordered to pay a
fine to the owner. 1680. Any enslaved person leaving the
master's property needed a pass signed by the master. [15][16]
[17][18][19][20]

## 6. 1705.

Thanks to the Slave Codes, the enslaved are officially
classified as "property" and "real estate." They are the
equivalent of a chair or table, another indicator of wealth
**(See #13, #25)**. *They are also no longer considered human,
making it easier to do as you please to "inanimate objects."* At
the same time, the first formal slave patrols **(See #14, #15,
#22)** are organizing in the Carolina colonies. These
patrols have three primary functions: (1) Chase,
apprehend, and return any runaway enslaved persons to
their owners. (2) Provide a form of organized terror to
deter slave revolts, and (3) Maintain strict discipline
among the enslaved on plantations. These patrols spread
to every slave state and eventually became a foundation
for ... **(See #22)**. [21]

## 7. 1706-1721.

Scientist, Salem witch trial overseer, and Puritan minister
Cotton Mather is given a "gift" by his church –

an enslaved African named **Onesimus**. *Onesimus means "useful."* Mather teaches him to read and write, and, in return, Onesimus teaches him a life-saving medical technique everyone in Africa already knew – *"People take juice of small-pox and cutty skin, and putt in a drop"* – Onesimus is describing the practice of rubbing pus from an infected person into an open wound so the body could learn to fight it, now known as inoculation. Fifteen years later, a ship will arrive from the West Indies with more enslaved individuals and a virus. Boston, now suffering heavily from a smallpox outbreak, needs help. Mather begins promoting what Onesimus taught him. He even enlists the help of a physicist named Zabdiel Boylston, who tests Onesimus's technique on his own kids and two enslaved people. It works. The two try to promote it again, but Bostonians think they are absolutely crazy. [22] [23] Although their science confirms Onesimus is right again and again, they will have to wait another 75 years for their recognition **(See #15)**. Onesimus will wait for 220 years **(See #95)**.

**8. 1739-1740. The Stono Rebellion.**

In late August, the British colony of South Carolina announces the Security Act, which required all White men to carry their firearms to church on Sunday in case of a slave revolt or runaways. This act was passed in direct response to rival nation Spain's recent declaration of freedom to all runaway slaves, which resulted in the successful escape of at least 70 Africans from South Carolina to Spanish Florida last year.

And now, fears of revolts, runaways, and rebellions were rising. Two weeks after the act is passed, an enslaved Angolan named **Jemmy (See #17, #20)** gathers 20 enslaved Africans near the Stono River, less than 20 miles away from Charlestown (Charleston). Likely inspired by the runaway success, the group finalizes their plans to kill everyone in town and run away to Spanish Florida. On September 9, Jemmy's band of enslaved men and women break into a store, kill two shopkeepers, and steal weapons and gunpowder. There was no turning back now. Armed and bloodied, they burn down houses and kill more Whites. With fire and smoke rising high across the Carolina landscape, Jemmy's band of rebels grows from 20 to 100 as they boldly march down the road, waving banners, shouting "liberty," and beating a drum to signal other enslaved people to rebellion and freedom. William Bull and a small group of White planters were riding along the same road and saw the group from a distance. Realizing what was happening, Bull and his outnumbered companions immediately turned their horses, sounding the alarm as they went. After hearing Bull's alarm, dozens of armed White men rushed out of church. Nearby, Jemmy's band was resting in a large field, enjoying a moment of freedom, but they were unexpectedly interrupted by gunfire. Jemmy's group fired a few shots back, but 14 slaves were killed in the end, and another 30 had escaped to the countryside amidst the confusion. A manhunt went on for weeks as slave patrols and hired Native

Americans roamed the area to find the runaways.
Eventually, all the Africans were captured and
executed or returned to slavery. The Stono Rebellion
changed the institution of slavery in South Carolina
and across the other colonies as well. So much so that
South Carolina quickly passed new laws to limit any
new revolts. Largely blaming the rebellion on the fact
that the rebels were African, not American-born
Negros, the colony banned the importation of new
enslaved Africans for 10 years. Secondly, slave owners
were penalized for imposing excessive work and brutal
punishments. Thirdly, schools were instructed to teach
Christian doctrine to the enslaved. Fourthly,
plantations were now required to keep a ratio of one
White man for every 10 enslaved individuals. Last and
fifthly, the state passed the Negro Act **(See #38, #45)**,
which prohibited enslaved Blacks from growing their
own food, assembling in groups, earning money, or
learning to read **(See #26, #36, #37)**. [24] [25] [26] [27] *This law
ensured dependency and illiteracy and stopped income and
wealth.*

## 9. 1773-1777.

Twenty years after being captured in West Africa, sold
into slavery at seven or eight years old, shipped to
Boston and auctioned into the Wheatley family house,
young Phillis Wheatley is caught writing on a wall in
the house. Instead of being punished and whipped, the
family actually encourages and teaches her to read and
write, leading to her first book of poetry. After traveling
to London with the Wheatley's, the Countess

of Huntingdon publishes her collection of writings entitled *Poems on Various Subjects, Religious and Moral.* Phillis becomes the first African American and enslaved American to publish a book of poetry. [28] In other news, back in America, the first 120 enslaved Africans has grown to 37,000, and the Revolutionary War begins in 1775. American-born colonists fight against the British Crown. *I'm sure you remember that whole bit about "no taxation without representation" from school.* Looking for extra help, the Brits declare that any enslaved persons willing to fight for them would be freed. 20,000 join the Crown while 5,000-8,000 "join" the colonists in their fight for… freedom? [29] [30] **(See #19, #28, #31, #39, #44, #54, #58, #61, #84, #87, #100).** *Relevant when we get to the War of 1812 and a certain poem in 37 years* **(See #19).**

**10. 1776. "Independence" Day.**

While the war is still being fought for another seven years, the Declaration of Independence is John Hancock'd by 56 signatories. *Hancock was the first guy to sign the document, which is why his name is still famous.* The document becomes a symbolic and literal metaphor for freedom and independence. *But allow me to reiterate: 37,000 enslaved people watched those freedom fireworks from slave cabins. And now you hopefully understand the difference in celebratory opinion regarding the 4th of July.* **(See #25, #51).** However, despite what that paper declared, all men are NOT created equal. Life, Liberty, and the Pursuit of Happiness are NOT for everyone. It's specifically for White men with land and property. The enslaved are obvious but poor, landless White men and all White women are also included in the "not created equal" section. [31] [32] *Now we have the founding of hegemony, classism, and White male privilege. This period is also the subtle beginnings of White supremacist ideals held by propertyless, lower-class White men. Although they had no land and were not among the middle and upper-class Whites, what they did have and own was their Whiteness. No matter their monetary status, it was the one thing that would forever maintain their superiority over Blacks.*

## 11. 1777-1787.

After Massachusetts becomes the first state to institutionalize slavery **(See #3)**, independent Vermont [33] and the state of Pennsylvania become the first two states to abolish it. **The Quakers (See #14, #17, #20, #97)**, who made it illegal amongst themselves to own any enslaved person, presses the state governments to end slavery. [34] [35] Obviously, they ignore their feather-inked letters. In response, the Quakers begin organizing a secret network throughout the south to help the enslaved run away to northern states and on to freedom. This network will later be known as **the Underground Railroad (See #14, #24, #97)**. [36] Following Vermont and Pennsylvania, New Hampshire (1783), Massachusetts (1783), and Rhode Island (1784) also abolish slavery. [37] The Northwest Ordinance of 1787 also ensured slavery would not exist in the new and future states of Ohio (1803), Indiana (1816), Illinois (1818), Michigan (1837), Wisconsin (1848), and Minnesota (1858). [38] Despite the radical move, all these states will find themselves in a particularly compromising situation in a few years **(See #13)**.

**12. 1789. The Supreme Court.**

The Judiciary Act of 1789 creates the Supreme Court. This body of all-White men *(at least until 1981, when Sandra Day O'Connor is added as the first female justice)* will go on to shape the course of American history for the next 233 years **(See #25, #36, #38, #53, #55, #60, #62, #69, #72, #73, #80, #99, #100)**. Meanwhile, 44-year-old U.S. Ambassador to France (and recent widow), Thomas Jefferson, begins his "relationship" with **Sally Hemings**, his 14-year-old enslaved house servant. Hemings bears Jefferson seven children, of which only four would survive: Beverly, Harriet, Madison, and Eston. [39] They will remain enslaved "with executive privilege" for at least another 36 years **(See #21)**.

**13. Also in 1789. Three-Fifth's A Human.**

The brand new Congress passes the Constitution of the United States and agrees to the **3/5 Compromise**. Large slave states wanted representation based on total population, and smaller slave states wanted each state to have the same number of representatives. Congress compromises, so the House of Representatives will be based on population and the Senate will have two reps per state. This is the origins of our current government structure. But one major question lingers: to count the enslaved or not count the enslaved? Remember, they are considered property **(See #6, #8, #25)**, so how can they be counted within the non-propertied human population? Of course, the enslaved south wanted them all to be counted – the more people, the more seats in the House. But this left the north at an unfair advantage and politically disadvantaged for doing the right thing by gradually abolishing slavery **(See #11)**. Thus the 3/5 Compromise: the enslaved will now be counted for population AND political representation. 40 Here's how this worked. At the time, Virginia had the largest population and political influence. In 1790, Virginia's population was about 748,000. 442,000 were White people and 293,000 were enslaved. Three-fifths of 293,000 equals 175,800, so that number was added to the total population of White people **(442,000)**, an overall total of 617,800. This inhumane math calculation sets the foundation for the Electoral College **(See #17, #94)** and the reason the south had a significantly disproportionate influence on the presidency and the nation for about 76 years until 1865. So much influence in fact, that out of the 12 presidents who owned enslaved persons, seven were from Virginia.

**14. 1790-1793.**

The first-ever U.S. Census is captured, and in less than 300 years, the enslaved population in America has

300 years, the enslaved population in America has grown tremendously. Results: Out of 3.9 million people, 700,000 are enslaved. Remember, it was 37,000 just 15 years ago **(See #9)**, and it's nowhere near finished growing. [41] Congress passes the Residence Act and debates on where to put its new house, capitol, and capital - which is currently known as Federal City, but will later be renamed to the City of Washington and then re-renamed to the District of Columbia (D.C.). After deciding on a new home, 300,000 enslaved persons are brought in from the Maryland-Virginia area for a very important job: building the White House **(See #17, #19, #89)**. [42][43][44] *Just before the construction begins, the original architect, Pierre L'Enfant, is fired by George Washington. Benjamin Ellicott is hired and asks free American African mathematician, surveyor, clockmaker, and astronomer* **Benjamin Banneker** *to help survey and design the city plans. In summary, Black people built and designed D.C., the White House, the Capitol, and at least 13 other monuments.* [45][46] Those that were not involved in construction were running away. The gradual increase in runaways to free states forced enslavers to lobby Congress to pass the first Fugitive Slave Act of 1793 **(See #24, #32)**. [47][48] This law provides legal authority to slave patrols to capture runaway enslaved persons **(See #6, #15, #22)**, enables the kidnapping of free Black men (known as "blackbirding") - *Example: The capture of free Black New Yorker* **Solomon Northup**, *the author and subject of 12 Years a Slave* [49][50][51] - and makes it a federal

crime to help runaways. In response, Whites and Blacks in the North create anti-slave vigilance committees to protect those running away, while the now federally criminal Quakers **(See #11, #24, #97)** increase their secret Underground Railroad activities. *For 72 more years, all American Africans are enslaved people until proven free.*

## 15. 1793-1796.

Inventor Eli Whitney invents the Cotton Gin, a device which separates the seeds from the cotton. 52 The gin is short for "engine." Because this invention speeds up the process of picking cotton, Whitney thought this would reduce the need for slaves. *The naivete of this man! Au contraire!* The rapid expansion of cotton production brings a rapid increase in African importation. Before the cotton gin, it took one enslaved individual 10 hours to produce one pound of cotton. Now, three enslaved persons can handle 50 pounds in one day. *Due to this increased production, southern slave owners have guaranteed wealth, and the American economy has guaranteed income, which is extremely important in 70 more years when all this money faces the risk of going away* **(See #26)**. Two years later, George and Martha Washington's favorite enslaved house servant, **Oney Judge**, escapes from the President's House in New York. While she's on the run in New Hampshire, Washington places ads in the paper, hires slave patrols, and even uses his presidential powers to seek help from federal officials. She lives her entire life in hiding but is never found. [53] [54]

Seventy-five years later, Cotton Mather and Zabdiel Boylston **(See #7)** finally receive their posthumous scientific credit for the "discovery" of inoculation after Edward Jenner's work with cow pus becomes popular. *Let's wait another 145 years for some real recognition, shall we?* **(See #95)**.

**16. 1779.**

The Haitian-born, French-educated, and U.S.-raised **Jean-Baptiste Point du Sable** settles down with his family and builds a trading post in the not-even-a-state-yet-region of Eschecagou, Illinois. He is the first Black man and the first person to do so. The visitors who came to his shop always mispronounced the area's name. They called it "Chicago." *This story becomes relevant again in 227 years* **(See #88)**. [55]

**17. 1800-1804.**

After eight years of free enslaved labor, the White House is finally complete, and the President's House is moved to the swamplands of D.C. **(See #14, #19, #89)**. *And they will have to build it again in 14 years* **(See #19)**. At the same time, three hours away in Richmond, Virginia, an enslaved man named **Gabriel Prosser** is channeling his inner Jemmy **(See #8, #20)**. Believing himself called by God, he organizes a plot to kill all Whites except Quakers, Methodists, and Frenchmen. Gabriel meets with other enslaved men under the guise of holding religious meetings, but two of the men who've been attending the meetings inform their masters of what's been discussed. These masters reveal the plot known as "Gabriel's Conspiracy" to the rest of the town, and 26 men, including Gabriel, are found guilty and hanged. The plan was one of the most feared insurrectionists' plots in history. Just like South Carolina after the Stono Rebellion **(See #8)**, all slave states now forbid Blacks from holding religious meetings at night. [56] Meanwhile, Congress makes a 12th Amendment to the Constitution and ensures that electors designate their votes for president and vice president. They also make tie- breaking rules: The House of Reps breaks the president's vote and the Senate breaks the vice president's. This ruling is the beginning of the Electoral College **(See #13, #94)**. [57][58]

**18. 1807-1808. The American Slave Trade.**

Because it's quite the conundrum to justify being a Christian and an enslaver or overseer, the Christian missionaries in London for the Society for the Conversion of Negro Slaves invents the "Parts of the Holy Bible, Selected for the Use of the Negro Slaves, in the British West India Islands." Whew! That was a "she sells seashells by the seashore" type of mouthful. They called it **"The Slave Bible"** for short **(See #21)**. The book's stated purpose is to "improve" the lives of the enslaved. *How mighty Christian of them.* This bible is extremely redacted and includes only 10% of the Old Testament, half of the New Testament, and scriptures highlighting servitude like Ephesians 6:5 — "Servants, be obedient to them that are your masters." [59]

Any stories which would stir escape are removed, like Exodus 5:1, when Moses says, "Let my people go." Anything saying everyone is equal under Jesus is scratched, like Galatians 3:28, which says, "There is neither Jew nor Greek, slave nor free, male nor female, for you are all one in Christ Jesus." Additionally, the entire book of Revelations is gone. [60] And while the enslaved in America are getting a brand new bible, the U.S. government is finally banning all importation of Africans for slavery. *On paper, not in practice.* After 282 years of legal African human trafficking, illegal African human smuggling and auctioning becomes the trend, and the American internal slave trade begins. Now that Africans cannot be legally trafficked across the Atlantic, the Lower (Deep) South territories and states of modern day South Carolina, Georgia, Alabama, Mississippi, and Louisiana establishes a domestic human trade agreement with the Upper (Still) South regions of modern day North Carolina, Tennessee, Virginia, Kentucky, and West Virginia to purchase from one another. State economies flourish, especially for states like Virginia and South Carolina, which own a significant number of enslaved persons. [61][62] There was so much traffic in South Carolina that Charleston was known as the **"Ellis Island for African Slaves"** because it was the nation's slave trade capital and 40% of enslaved Africans brought into the country passed through the Charleston Harbor.

## 19. 1812-1816. Star-Spangled Origins.

The War of 1812, a.k.a. the American Revolution Part 2. [63][64] The war is actually supposed to be between the Brits and Napoleon's France, but because the U.S. is selling supplies to both sides, the Brits turn their military attention to the west. *I mean, if I'm fighting someone, and you're giving them extra gloves to fight me, I gotta fight you too!* More than 5,000 American Africans join the fight for...freedom? **(See #9, #28, #31, #39, #44, #54, #58, #61, #84, #87, #100).** [65] In year two of the fight (1814), the Brits burn down two buildings the enslaved had just built, the White House and the Capitol building **(See #14, #17, #89).** *The riots on January 6, 2021, was only the second time in history this place had been attacked* **(See #98).** They also bomb Fort McHenry in Baltimore, Maryland. On the night of the bombing, a slave-owning lawyer named **Francis Scott Key** is detained on a British ship watching the attack. Congress sent him there to negotiate with the Brits to free an American doctor, but the Brits tell him he must stay put until the morning. And from his ship quarters, he watches the British Navy bomb the fort. By morning, he is inspired by an American flag still waving. [66] *The same American flag that was stitched by an enslaved woman named* **Grace Wisher.** [67] So inspired, he writes a 4-stanza poem about it called "Defence of Fort M'Henry." [68][69] We know the first stanza by heart, but here's his little-known third stanza: "No refuge could save the hireling and slave / From the terror of flight or the gloom of the grave." *Translation: The stanza takes jabs at the enslaved who were killed trying to run to the British for freedom during the war.*

*Quick sidenote to remedy any confusion: We only sing the first stanza of the four because the U.S. dropped the other three during World War I out of respect for its new best friend - Great Britain. Nevertheless, this poem will become a fiery focal point of debate and protests in exactly 202 years* **(See #94)**. After the war, Key provides his lawyer services to enslavers looking to retrieve their escaped persons. Meanwhile, the poem he wrote on the ship is later retitled **"The Star-Spangled Banner"** and makes its way through newspapers across the nation **(See #51)**. Meanwhile, four years later in 1818, **Frederick Augustus Washington Bailey** is born into slavery in Talbot County, Maryland **(See #22, #23, #25, #49)**.

**20. 1820-1822.**

Four years after Bailey is born, **Araminta "Minty" Ross (See #23, #24, #27, #43)** is also born into slavery in Dorchester County, Maryland. This is the same year the American Colonization Society of Quakers, Slaveholders, and Politicians begin sending free Blacks to Liberia, Africa. [70] *Yup, free American Blacks founded Liberia. The name derives from the Latin word "liber" - free.* The belief was that Blacks and Whites could never live together equally, and the few free Black people that lived in America would undermine the entire institution of slavery. [71] *Because enslaved individuals seeing free Black individuals walk about stirs the mind for their own freedom.* Meanwhile, the enslaved and freed Blacks of South Carolina are now required to wear distinctive identification tags. **Denmark Vessey** says to hell with slavery and his enslaved identification and like his rebellious ancestral predecessor Jemmy **(See #8, #17)**, he too organizes a massive revolt but is executed with 40 others. [72] And in Virginia, 22-year-old **Nat Turner** is having his first spiritual visions of blood-stained corn, hieroglyphics, and Black and White ghosts fighting in the sky. He is convinced that the **"great day of judgment is at hand."** [73]

**21. 1825-1828. The Birth of the Black Stereotype.**

One year after Seneca Village - *or known today as Central Park* - **(See #84)** becomes the first free Black town in New York, [74] Thomas Jefferson dies at the age of 83. The children he had with Sally Hemings **(See #15)** are freed, but with one stipulation: they must forever deny their father's identity. Because of their fair features, they "pass" into society and are documented as "Free White People." Sally Hemings, on the other hand, never receives her freedom. She is passed on to Jefferson's oldest daughter, Martha, and is allowed to live "freely" on Monticello Plantation in Charlottesville, Virginia **(See #96)**. [75] *City-wide house arrest was quite the privilege.* Two years later, New York-born traveling stage actor **Thomas D. Rice (See #83, #84, #97)** takes what he sees in the south, grossly exaggerates it, and makes "Black Face" and "Jumping Jim Crow" minstrel famous at a show in Louisville, Kentucky. His shows give birth to the enduring negative Black stereotypes of: The Sambo. Jim Crow. The Savage. The Mammy and Aunt Jemima **(See #40, #47, #97)**. The Sapphire and Jezebel. The lazy, chicken and watermelon, big smiling subservient yet illiterate house slave **(See #24)**. And the hypersexualized lusting and rapist deviant **(See #43, #46, #47, #51, #58, #83)**. [76 77 78 79]

While stereotypes are created on stage and accepted as truth in the fields, the Slave Bible **(See #18)** spreads throughout the country. At the same time **Scientific Racism** - the belief that Whites were mentally superior and Blacks were inferior and more akin to monkeys - and **Phrenology** - the pseudoscience which studied the measurement of bumps on the skull to predict mental traits - racially concluded that Blacks had smaller skulls than Whites, which therefore solidified their "inferior" status throughout the world. *If you've ever seen the movie Django Unchained, it's the scene where Leonardo DiCaprio's character, Calvin Candie, monologues while holding "Old Uncle Ben's" skull. If you haven't seen it, well, forget I mentioned this or find it on YouTube.* The bible and the science become a sigh of relief for enslavers because they provide justifications for slavery while providing them "scientific" differences between races to fall back on comfortably. It also offers overseers and regular citizens who do not own enslaved persons a justification for their racial superiority over Blacks in general, thus adding to their belief of their place in the world. [80] [81] [82] *"See, I'm not a bad person. You were born to be this way — to be inferior — and thus enslaved. It is simply my God-given duty to help you improve your status." The enslavers ideology is what the Slave Bible, Phrenology, and Scientific Racism do. They take away the individual ownership and replace it with a "White Savior" mentality, which is why many slave owners prided themselves on "being good people" who "looked after their slaves" and "treated them like family."*

## 22. 1835-1836.

An angry mob captures an enslaved man named **Mcintosh** for allegedly killing a deputy sheriff. He is chained to a tree, burned to death, and lynched in front of 1,000 bystanders in St. Louis, **becoming the first recorded lynching on record**. In the same year, the first police department is established in Boston, followed by New York (1845) and Chicago (1851). It's 130 years later and slave patrols **(See #6, #14, #15)** still police the enslaved south. [83][84][85] *Remember their role: Chase and apprehend. Organize terror. Maintain discipline. This will be relevant throughout the entirety of history and way too many numbers to see.* While those patrols are searching for their next victim, **Anna Murray**, a free Black Maryland woman, inspires Frederick Bailey to escape his enslavement and provides him with a sailor's uniform and part of her savings to help. Four trains, one steamboat, and less than 24 hours later, Bailey is a free man in New York. Fearful of recapture, Frederick changes his last name to Douglass. Eleven days later, he proposes to that same lady who helped him to freedom and makes Anna his wife **(See #19, #23, #25, #27, #28, #29, #49)**. [86] Back west, hundreds of volunteers like slave-trading Jim Bowie, former Tennessee politician Davy Crockett, and Alabama fugitive William B. Travis die in defense of the Alamo in San Antonio, Texas in March 1836.

*Travis' enslaved manservant Joe fought and survived the battle of the Alamo after a Mexican officer told his men not to kill him. Joe is the main reason we know so much about its history today.* One month later, the remaining Texas volunteers defeat Santa Anna's Mexican army, securing independence for the new republic. Sam Houston is named president and slavery is officially codified in the Texas Constitution for the next 29 years **(See #30)**. *"All persons of color who were slaves for life previous to their emigration to Texas, and who are now held in bondage, shall remain in the like state of servitude..."*

**23. 1844-1845.**

Although still enslaved, Minty marries a free Black man named John Tubman and the 24-year-old now goes by **Harriet (See #20, #24, #27, #43)**. A few months later, she hires a lawyer to investigate her family history and discovers her mother had been freed before her birth by a technicality. Meaning she should have been born free. *Remember Elizabeth Key* **(See #4)** *and the Hereditary Slave Codes of 1662* **(See #5)**, *the child takes after the mother's status.* The lawyer advises her to drop the case because no one will hear it, and it will be difficult to prove. She does, but is more than angry because she has had to live a life enslaved for 24 years. Her dreams of freedom change her forever. While plotting her freedom, fellow Marylander and the recently free Frederick Douglass publishes his autobiography, *Narrative of the Life of Frederick Douglass, an American Slave*, which bolsters anti-slave sentiment in the north and gradually helps improve the status of Black life **(See #27, #29)**.

**24. 1848-1852.**

It must be runaway season because as Harriet plots and Frederick writes, **William and Ellen Craft** make one of the most daring escapes from their plantation in Macon, Georgia, just three days before Christmas. [87] Ellen was born a quadroon, a person who is 25% Black and looks White, thanks to master-enslaved "relations." Using this to her advantage, she disguises herself as a rich, White male while her husband, William, who is 100% Black, acts as her enslaved manservant. After multiple segregated train rides and steamships, the Craft's finally arrive in Philadelphia on Christmas Day and burst into tears - they are free. *See the Craft's autobiography, Running A Thousand Miles to Freedom.* Back in Maryland, Harriet Tubman **(See #20, #23, #27, #43)** is finalizing the plans for her escape. This comes after receiving the news that her two brothers will be sold to another plantation, and her husband keeps threatening to sell her. After failing to persuade her brothers to leave with her and not risking being sold by John, Harriet leaves alone, making her way to Philadelphia and freedom. The next year, in 1850, she courageously goes back to Maryland to rescue her sister and her sister's family. This is only the beginning. [88] [89] This is the same year, Jasper Newton "Jack" Daniel is born in Lynchburg, Tennessee, the same area soon-to-be Confederate General **Nathan Bedford Forrest** will do much of his post-war "recruiting" in a few years **(See #32, #43)**. *Eight years from now, Jasper's* *family will send him to Dan Call's farm to work and learn a new trade from an unlikely source* **(See #25, #29, #96)**. [90] Two years after Harriet escapes, an enslaved man from Louisa County, Virginia, plots his escape after his master lied to him and sold his wife and child to another plantation. **Henry "Box" Brown** patiently saved up enough earnings and paid $86.00 (about $2,643 today) to mail himself to Philadelphia IN A WOODEN CRATE. [91] Twenty-seven hours and 275 miles later, a box labeled "dry goods" arrives at its intended designation. *"If you've never been deprived of your liberty, you cannot realize the power of that hope of freedom" – Henry Brown*. Two years later, Dr. Samuel Cartwright, a proponent of scientific racism **(See #21)**, attempts to explain the reasoning behind the increase in runaways, which was thanks to the Underground Railroad **(See #11, #14, #97)** and the Fredericks', Harriets', Williams, Ellens', and Henry Box Browns' of the world. He proclaims the enslaved are suffering from a mental illness called "drapetomania," which makes them escape, and that free Blacks in the north suffered from far more mental illnesses than their enslaved counterparts. [92] The number of runaways also contributes to Congress passing the Second Fugitive Slave Act of 1850 **(See #14, #32)**, which strengthens the rights of enslavers. [93] The next year, **Sojourner Truth** ask the Women's Rights Convention in Akron, Ohio – **"Ain't I a Woman?"** when demanding equal rights for Black women. [94] Harriet Beecher Stowe also publishes her widely successful, southern-loathed book **(See #43)** *Uncle*

*Tom's Cabin*. In the novel version, Uncle Tom sacrifices himself for two enslaved women who run away after their master plans to sexually abuse them, but directors of stage and film adaptations distort this character for White audiences, portraying him as an old man with poor English and one who will sell out any Black man to gain favor with his White master or mistress. *Think (or YouTube) Django Unchained again and Samuel L. Jackson's character, the house servant Stephen*. Theatrical versions of Uncle Tom stirred a legacy of debate, especially against Black males considered to be nonviolent, compassionate, subservient, and overly considerate of White interests at the expense or risk of Black progress **(See #43, #69)**. [95] [96] While Harriet Stowe is gaining literary success, the escaped-slave-autobiographic-writing-now-popular-abolitionist-speaker Frederick Douglass **(See #19, #22, #28, #29, #49)** disdainfully asks an all-White audience in Rochester, New York: **"What, to the Slave, is the 4th of July?" (See #10, #51)**. *Again, two very different histories and two very different celebrations, or lack thereof, on this day.* [97] Meanwhile, Douglass's friend and *North Star* newspaper co-founder **Martin Robison Delany (See #28, #43, #44, #71)** has just completed a very different manifesto. *The Condition, Elevation, Emigration, and Destiny of the Colored People of the United States, Politically Considered* calls for Black emigration from the United States to Liberia and Central America. It is viewed as a decisive break from Douglass's gradual mainstream abolitionist movement to freedom and signals the **birth of Black nationalist separatism**. [98]

*This idea will be revived again in 64 more years* **(See #44)** *and again in 114 years* **(See #71)**. This is the same time frame that Charles B. Allen is founding the secret Nativists society known as The Order of the Star Spangled Banner in New York City. The group is established to protest the rise of Irish, Catholic, and German immigration and is looking to restore their vision of what America should look like: all White, all male, and all Protestant. They eventually form into The Know Nothings, the third largest political party in American history. The Order spreads their anti-immigration, anti-Catholicism, and anti-Black ideas throughout the country while sowing the seeds for racists and segregationist ideologies **(See #31, #38, #43, #45)**, laws **(See #25, #31, #38, #83)**, extremely violent hate groups **(See #32, #43, #48, #62, #94)**, and extremely violent acts **(See #39, #45, #46, #47, #50, #51, #57, #70, #96, #97)**. All embedded within the fears of being replaced. *And herein lies the origins of the* **Great Replacement Theory**.

**25. 1855-1857. The Dreadful Dred Scott Decision.**

Booker **(See #30, #37, #40, #41, #43, #46)** is born enslaved on a plantation in Franklin County, Virginia, just in time for the monumental ***Dred Scott v. Sanford*** decision **(See #33, #37, #70)**. Dred Scott was an enslaved man who sued for his freedom because his owner took him to live in states where slavery was illegal. He lost. And the Supreme Court decides 7-2 that Blacks were property, they could NEVER be human or citizens **(See #6, #8)**, and therefore had no grounds to sue anyone, especially a White person. [99] [100] *This case will be the law of the land for more than 100 years* (**See #33, #70**). Elsewhere, on a farm in Tennessee, **Uncle Nathan Nearest Green**, an enslaved man on Dan Call's farm, meets the young Jasper "Jack" Newton. Call, who makes his living as a preacher, grocer, and whiskey seller, sees some promise in Jasper and tells him he will learn the whiskey business. But Call doesn't have time to instruct him, so he passes him off to "the best whiskey maker" on his plantation — Nathan Green. And he's the best for a reason. His whiskey talents are based on traditional African recipes (**See #24, #29, #96**).

**26. 1860. The Peak of American Enslavement.**

Four million enslaved Blacks are valued at over approximately four billion dollars. Slavery makes the **Enslaved States of America** one of the wealthiest places in the world. Thanks to the cotton gin (**See #15**), 75% of the world's cotton comes from the U.S., making the country the number one distributor of cotton. [101] [102] [103] [104] *In fact, if all the enslaved states combined themselves into an actual country, it would've been the fourth wealthiest country in the world.* **Abraham Lincoln** versus Stephen Douglas. Lincoln was against slavery, but he did not believe Blacks were equal to Whites. During a debate against Douglas on September 18, 1858, he said, "I will say then that I am not, nor ever have been, in favor of bringing about, in any way, the social and political equality of the White and Black races." [105][106] He leaned on those remarks heavily, especially when campaigning in the South, because he knew he needed the pro-slavery votes. In the end, Abraham Lincoln wins the 1860 presidential election against Douglas, and it immediately stirs geographic trouble. In response to his victory, 11 states secede from the U.S. and form the **Confederate States of America (CSA)**. Lincoln had no plans of ending slavery. He just did not want it to expand to the new western territories. But that didn't matter. The CSA names Jefferson Davis as its president and moves its capital three hours away from D.C. to Richmond, Virginia - the number two slave trade state in the country (South Carolina was #1) and the same city Gabriel Prosser tried to bring down 60 years ago **(See #17)**. [107] The CSA sees Lincoln as a real threat to their billion-dollar enterprise, which is the reason Article 1, Section 9 of the CSA Constitution reads: "No bill of attainder, ex post facto law, or law denying or impairing the right of property in Negro slaves shall be passed." [108] *Translation: Slavery will never be illegal, and we are willing to fight and die for it. Feel free to use that should you find yourself in a Confederate Flag "heritage, not hate" debate.*

## 27. 1861. The American Civil War.

April 12-13. The Confederate army storms a Union army base at Fort Sumter, South Carolina, and the Civil War begins for money and slavery - not "states' rights." [109][110]

*Should you find yourself in a debate with someone who*

*believes it was over states rights, ask them a simple question:*
*The states right to do what exactly?* Harriet Tubman **(See**
**#20, #23, #24, #43)**, with a $40,000 bounty on her head,
makes her 19th and last trip into the south to rescue the
enslaved. She then works with the Union Army setting
up a network of spies and scouts, gathering information
to disrupt Confederate supply lines, and leading raids
on plantations. Elsewhere across the battlefields, the
enslaved are running away from plantations, taking
advantage of the early fighting. Taking advice from
Frederick Douglass, Lincoln takes note of the many
runaways arriving at Union camps and begins drafting
a historic document. As the war starts in the south,
Emperor Napoleon III has just landed his French forces
across the border in Veracruz, Mexico. He's there to
establish a new French colony after his uncle, Napoleon
I, lost Haiti after the enslaved won their freedom
during the Haitian Revolution (1804). Haiti was the
richest French colony in the world at the time, and now
the nephew has plans to make him proud by expanding
the French empire while the U.S. is distracted. [111] [112]

**28. 1862.**

Lincoln knows he can't afford to fight both the south
and France. This is one of the main reasons he allows
the border states of Kentucky, Maryland, Delaware, and
Missouri to keep their enslaved in the Union. But
thankfully, he won't have to worry about France
because on May 5th (Cinco de Mayo), Napoleon's
forces are defeated by General Ignacio Zaragoza's

outnumbered ragtag forces at the Battle of Puebla. [113] *Butterfly Effect Moment: France ends up winning their war in Mexico overall, but this small defeat changes Napoleon's plans and keeps history in check. Had the French won that battle, they were planning to use Puebla as a support base to provide the Confederate Army with weapons for cotton. And if that happens, who knows how the Civil War plays out. Potential plot twists: Robert E. Lee makes Ulysses S. Grant and the north surrender. Lincoln is forced to resign and lives out his days as a traitor. John Wilkes Booth lives on to be the greatest actor of his time. Richmond, Virginia, becomes the U.S. capitol with Jefferson Davis as president. The northern states agree to never secede from the Confederate States of America and are forced to reinstate their slave laws. Slavery keeps going for who knows how long, and Blacks remain enslaved until another civil war happens. Unfortunately, the French regroup to take Puebla one year later, but that's how significant the victory on Cinco de Mayo was for the U.S. Civil War.* Meanwhile, back on the battlefields in America, Lincoln realizes he needs more men. So, remembering all those runaways and all those critiques from Frederick Douglass, he does something incredibly radical for the time. He allows Black men to sign up to fight in the war. Almost 200,000 Black men join the fight for... freedom? **(See #9, #19, #31, #39, #44, #54, #58, #61, #84, #87, #100).** [114] [115] *This is an opportunity to gain revenge, but more so to prove they are capable. And even more to prove they are human* **(See #25).** Black soldiers show up and show out. Deciding not to go to Liberia or Central America, the Father of Black Nationalism

Martin Delany **(See #24, #44, #71)** becomes the first Black field officer in the U.S. Army. The 54th Colored Regiment of Massachusetts Volunteers show their bravery. [116][117] *The movie Glory is based on this unit, starring Morgan Freeman, Matthew Broderick, and Denzel Washington's famous one-tear cry.* **Robert Smalls** steals a Confederate ship used to transfer cotton, the C.S.S. Planter, from the harbor in Charleston, South Carolina, and sails with 17 Black passengers to northern Union lines for freedom. [118] **Cathay Williams** changes her name to "William Cathy" and enlists in the Union Army to fight with the 39th Infantry Regiment, which will soon become **the Buffalo Soldiers (See #31).** *She is the first Black woman to enlist and the only known female Buffalo Soldier. Also, she is the second woman on record to serve in the U.S. Army after Deborah Sampson disguised herself as "Robert Shurtleff" during the Revolutionary War.* [119] And while the bullets are flying and cotton is being picked, **Ida Bell Wells** is born in Holly Springs, Mississippi, in the middle of a war for her future **(See #38, #40, #42, #46).** [120]

## 29. 1863-1864. Emancipation.

Lincoln's ideas about American Africans evolve. Before, he thought they did not deserve to vote, serve on juries, hold office, or intermarry. Now he's okay with limited voting rights and the full freedom for Black men to improve their condition in society and enjoy the fruits of their labor. *But still not intermarry. One thing at a time here, bucko.* [121][122]

Again, with Frederick Douglass in his ear, he signs the **Emancipation Proclamation** with an effective date of January 1, 1863. *Imagine the New Year's ball dropping across the plantations!* The institution of slavery ends *(on paper)* in the 11 Confederate rebel states—South Carolina, Mississippi, Florida, Alabama, Georgia, Louisiana, Texas, Virginia, Tennessee, Arkansas, and North Carolina— and frees *(on paper)* almost four million enslaved persons. However, slavery still exists *(in real life)* in Texas, Kentucky, Maryland, Delaware, and Missouri. [123] [124] And just in time for the emancipation celebrations, Jasper Newton Jack Daniel introduces his first batch of libations, Old No. 7 whiskey. Two years later, he will open the country's very first distillery. Even with their freedom, Nearest Green and his sons will go on to work with Jack becoming the first Black master distillers in America **(See #24, #25, #96).** [125] [126] *If you Google "Jack Daniels and Nearest Green," an incredible picture pops up. But the Black man sitting right next to Jack is not Nearest; it's his son George. The fact that George is that close, especially amongst the rest of the White men in the photo, alludes to his position within the company as someone of importance.*

**30. 1865. "What Does The Negro Want Most ... ?"**

After speaking to a group of Black reverends in Savannah, Georgia, famed Union Army General William T. "Sherman's March to the Sea" Sherman signs **Special Field Order 15** on January 16. Approved by Lincoln, the order allots

**400,000 acres of Confederate-confiscated land from South Carolina to Florida to thousands of formerly enslaved families.** [127][128] *Better known as "40 Acres and a Mule," but keep reading* **(See #31)**. Meanwhile, Union soldiers are still defeating Confederate armies, taking over plantations and freeing the enslaved. Booker is freed after Union soldiers arrive at his plantation near Franklin County, Virginia. Shedding the name of his enslaver, he takes the name of his stepfather and is forever known as **Booker T. Washington (See #25, #37, #40, #41, #43, #46).** [129] Four months later, popular stage actor and Confederate sympathizer John Wilkes Booth assassinates Abraham Lincoln at the Ford Theater in Washington D.C., just six days after Robert E. Lee surrenders his troops at Appomattox Court House, Virginia, effectively ending the Civil War. Between 620,000-850,000 fight and die, 40,000 of which were American African soldiers. [130] Two months later on June 19, Union General Gordon Granger arrives in Galveston, Texas and announces **General Order No. 3**. The last 200,000 enslaved people in Texas (and America) are now free. *This event comes to be known as Juneteenth* **(See #81, #100).** [131] In honor of the slain president, Lincoln's Republican Party passes **the 13th Amendment**. Slavery in every state is now "officially" abolished, but the fine print opened the door for a new type of bondage **(See #31)**. Inspired by the U.S. emancipation, French artist Frederic Bartholdi and anti-slave activist Edouard de Laboulaye hold a meeting in Versailles, France, to discuss giving the U.S. a gift **(See #37)**. But little do the French know, Lincoln's assassination is literally about to change everything. Southern sympathizer, enslaver, and new president, Andrew Johnson, gives the surrendered Confederates all their land back and directs them to rebuild their governments, so long as they promise never to secede again. *Butterfly Effect Moment: If John Wilkes Booth is captured at Lincoln's second inaugural address - incredible picture you should Google - and Lincoln is never assassinated, and Johnson never becomes president, what does Black "40 Acres" America look like post-enslavement?* And after everything Harriet Tubman did during the war, she never receives pay or official documentation that she had ever served.

*****

# DECONSTRUCTION

# CHAPTER II:
# 1866-1947

## Deconstruction and the Emergence of the New Negro

*For the first time in their lives, they were free. The toil, sweat, and labor would be their own, for their own, and on their own land. Every morning from here on would be different. They remembered those nights they prayed until their throat hurt and their knees ached. And finally...freedom. But something is changing. The president who freed them has been killed, and rumors spread that the new one is different. Very different. He even owned slaves himself. The Union soldiers knock on the doors one by one. Belongings are scattered in the middle of the road. Tears, screams, and heartbreaks are heard by the next town over. All they were given was five months of freedom for a lifetime of work. They were being permanently evicted.*

*After being sworn in, Andrew Johnson directed the seceded states to hold elections and reform their governments. Those same Confederates leaders who wanted to maintain slavery were rewarded with property, statues, and military bases honoring their generals, as well as political supremacy to maintain their superiority, and history books retelling of their glorious sacrifice for states' rights.*

*But for the American African, it was an era of dashed hopes amidst the potential of what freedom was supposed to bring. Emancipation ushered in the haunting illusion of freedom and progress. The Deconstruction Era signaled a new world of vengeful legal barriers, residential restrictions, and police and Klan violence to impede the upward mobility for Black people everywhere, but most especially in the south. The institution of slavery was rebranded into mass imprisonment and Black bodies turned into strange fruit while right hands were raised in the oath to fight the nation's wars. Fighting for the freedoms of others and receiving none themselves at home.*

*Through it all, they resisted and persisted. Their very existence became a defiant stance against the status quo of racism and discrimination. Their great exodus out of the south was a clear sign of their determination to create a new destiny they could call their own and, once and for all, prove they were indeed human.*

**This is the Deconstruction Era.**

**31. 1866. The Reconstruction and Jim Crow Era.**

The Civil War is over and America sets its sights on expanding the nation westward. The completion of the railroads to the West (by Chinese labor) opens vast areas of the region to settlement and economic development, nicely named **"Manifest Destiny"** in our history books. [132][133] This "destiny" also reignites the American Indian Wars for the next 25 years, which will see the removal of thousands of Natives from their tribal lands. More than 5,000 Blacks leftover from the Civil War, including the Buffalo Soldiers **(See #28)**, again join the fight for... freedom? **(See #9, #19, #28, #39, #44, #54, #58, #61, #84, #87, #100)**. [134][135] In D.C., Frederick Douglass is meeting with Andrew Johnson to continue the discussions he held with the recently assassinated Lincoln regarding the right for Black Americans to vote. But Johnson refuses, telling Douglass that granting Blacks suffrage would result in "great injury to the White as well as the colored man." After granting pardons to the Confederate soldiers, Johnson vetoes two bills designed to provide equal rights and economic and educational assistance to the ex-slaves and allows the south to rebuild themselves on their terms. [136] And those terms are underscored by the writings of journalist and Confederate sympathizer **Edward A. Pollard**. His books, *The Lost Cause: A New Southern History of the War of the Confederates* and *The Lost Cause Regained* **(See #38, #44, #45, #51)** focus on the reasons for Confederate secession, the legality of states' rights, and the benefits of slavery. [137] [138] *This alternate universe will become the foundation for southern recognition and representation by groups like the United Daughters of the Confederacy in 18 years* **(See #38)**. Meanwhile, the Jim Crow Era begins for the **Black and unlucky**. [139] [140] **Jim Crow and the Black Codes** were the post-emancipation replica of the Slave Codes **(See #5)** and the Negro Act **(See #8, #38)**. Southern states legalized the Black Codes to keep Blacks working for low wages, in severe debt, and restricted from owning property, conducting business, and buying or leasing land. [141] [142] [143] [144] *Are you keeping track of how long they have stopped wealth and kept the enslaved and free Black populations overly dependent on White authority and ownership? Believing the federal government had to protect the newly freed Black Americans, Lincoln's Republicans establish* **the Freedmen's Bureau**. [145] Most formerly enslaved persons literally had nowhere to go, so they stayed near the same areas and worked on the same lands they were just freed from, but now for an egregiously low minimum wage payment system known as **sharecropping**. [146] But those not sharecropping face a fate similar to their previous life because while everyone celebrated the passage of the 13th Amendment **(See #30)**, no one read the fine print —*"Neither slavery nor involuntary servitude, EXCEPT AS A PUNISHMENT FOR CRIME whereof the party shall have been duly convicted."*

*Translation: The institution of slavery is abolished, BUT prisoners can - and will - be treated as enslaved.*

## 32. Also in 1866.

The Fugitive Slave Acts of 1793 and 1850 **(See #14, #24)** evolve into the **Vagrancy Act of 1866**. [147] Former slave patrol bounty hunters receive their police officers' badges **(See #6, #19)** and are now charged with the capture of any Black man who looks "unemployed," "lazy," or "homeless." Black men who used to be black birded (kidnapped) and sold into slavery were still being black birded or falsely accused of some made-up crime and sold into prison. And what used to be known as chattel slavery is now known as the **Convict Leasing System, or "Slavery by Another Name."** This new system ensures that over 90% of the southern prison population is Black. [148 149 150 151] *This also becomes relevant when we get to the "Warmongering" era in 105 years* **(See #78)**. On more than one occasion, the slave patrol turned police officers join White ex-soldiers to exact revenge and kill free Black men, such as in the Memphis, Tennessee massacre that left 46 dead, 70 wounded, and several churches and schools burned. Two months later, the same thing happens in New Orleans, with 37 dead. [152] In the spirit of White vengeance, former Confederate General Nathan Bedford Forrest **(See #24, #43)** creates **the First Order of the Ku Klux Klan** in Pulaski, Tennessee. *It was not Indiana as popularly assumed, but at its peak, 40% of all White males in Indiana, including*

THE BLACK LIST: 1526 - 2022

*governors, politicians, businessmen, and religious leaders, were a part of the Klan.* Their goal is to reverse the new policies aimed at Black progression and seek political justice for crimes against White people by threatening Republican leaders and politicians. *The Great Replacers.* [153] Two years later, the Klan lives up to its stated purpose and assassinates George Ashburn, a Republican from Columbus, Georgia. [154]

## 33. 1867-1868.

Worried that Johnson is too sympathetic towards the south, Republicans divide the former Confederate states into five military districts and deploy Union troops to protect Black freedom, but it's short-lived **(See #36)**. Johnson's term ends in 1868, and **Union General Ulysses S. Grant** introduces himself as the new president by ratifying the **14th Amendment**. This act grants citizenship to all persons "born or naturalized in the United States," including formerly enslaved persons, and guarantees "equal protection under the laws." [155] *On paper, not in practice. Many believe this amendment would overturn the Dred Scott decision* **(See #25, #37, #70)**. *It most definitely did not. But it does become important in 75 years* **(See #48)** *and throughout the rest of history.* This is also the same year that **William Edward Burghardt Du Bois (See #37, #38, #40, #41, #42, #43, #49, #52, #68)** is born in Great Barrington, Massachusetts. And three years after freedom, John Willis Menard becomes the first Black American elected to the House of Representatives for Louisiana. He's also the first to give a speech to Congress. [156]

**34. 1869.**

32 years after the first Black college was founded in Pennsylvania (Cheyney University), Howard University School of Law becomes the first Black law school in the country. A few colleges integrated a sprinkling of Black students as early as 1823 (Alexander Lucius Twilight, Middlebury College, Vermont), 1826 (Edward A. Jones, Amherst College, and John Brown Russwurm, Bowdoin College), and the long list that graduated from Oberlin College in Ohio over the years. However, most predominantly White law schools and higher education universities had not yet made the broad leap to accepting Black applicants until the 1950s. [157] [158]

**35. 1870-1871.**

President Grant follows up the 14th with **the 15th Amendment,** which "guarantees" the right of U.S. citizens to vote will not be "denied or abridged on account of race." *On paper, not in practice.* [159] *But, just like the 14th, it too becomes important in 75 years* **(See #55)**. He also passes **the Enforcement Acts**, which made it a federal crime to interfere with Blacks' registration, voting, office holding, or jury service. *On what? Say it with me now! On paper, not in practice. Because it won't be effective, the government will be forced to pass this law again in 87 years* **(See #63)**. More than 5,000 people are indicted under these laws, and a little more than 1,000 are convicted.

The following year, Congress passes **the Ku Klux Klan Act,** which allows the government to act against terrorist organizations. *This act actually won't apply at all until a violent tragedy occurs to a particular person 94 years from now* **(See #70)**. Grant did not rigorously enforce these laws, but he does order the arrest of hundreds of Klan members. It doesn't matter because there is way too much support for the Klan, and convictions never happen. [160]

Two years after Menard makes history in the House, **Hiram Revels of Mississippi and Joseph Rainey of South Carolina** become the first Black Americans to serve in the Senate. [161] *Given the history we have discussed up to this point and after, these states are shocking, but this is clearly a direct reflection of the post-slavery Black political voting bloc.* Due to Black political potential, violent voter suppression increases throughout the South.

**36. 1875-1878. The Civil Rights Act of 1875.**

The Civil Rights Act of 1875 proclaims "equality of all men before the law" and tries to prohibit racial discrimination in public places. But, no. The Supreme Court overturns the bill with an 8-1 vote, ruling the act "unconstitutional." *We must wait about 89 years before this gets brought up again* **(See #69)**. [162] [163] [164] While the Supreme Court is being racist, President Rutherford B. Hayes adds to the troubles by dissolving the southern military districts after just eight years **(See #36)**. Removal of the Union soldiers from the former Confederate states allows the southern White Democrats (who will later refer to themselves as "Dixiecrats") who supported slavery and the Confederacy to begin changing the laws in their favor **(See #38)**. This is also the same time Black invention sparks. **Lewis Latimer**, the son of escaped slaves and former member of the U.S. Navy, lands a job sketching patents for $20.00 a week ($485.00 today). This leads him to one of his first patents, an improved toilet system for railroad cars, and being hired by Alexander Graham Bell to help sketch his new invention, the telephone. Three years later, Latimer teaches himself about electrical engineering and lighting and invents a carbon filament for light bulbs to help Black families afford electricity. Hearing about this invention, Latimer gets a call from Thomas Edison. He needs help with his light bulb and patent paperwork, copyright infringement protection, and running his library. Latimer agrees to help. *And the rest is history. Of course, Bell and Edison got all the historical credit, but now you know the man in the background who helped put the science together.* [165 166]

### 37. 1881-1886.

Just 16 years removed from slavery, Black folks are rapidly achieving, innovating, and succeeding. In Providence, Rhode Island, Black inventor **Philip Bell Downing** invents the street letter box - later called the mailbox. In Atlanta, Georgia, Black women are getting their higher education at the first college for Black women, Spelman University. In Tuskegee, Alabama, 25-year-old Booker T. Washington is now the president of Tuskegee Normal and Industrial Institute **(See #43, #51, #57)**. And in Nashville, Tennessee, W.E.B. Du Bois is a student at Fisk University, where he experiences southern racism for the first time, which changes his ideals for Black America forever. Elsewhere across America, long lines of people are waiting for their turn at the newest attraction at Whites-only carnivals and fairs. **The African Dodger, a.k.a. "Hit the Nigger Baby," a.k.a. "Hit the Coon,"** is the game in which White customers throw baseballs at Black people. *These are things you do to "objects" that are not human. Word to the Dred Scott Supreme Court* **(See #6, #25, #33, #70)**. The African Dodger also inspires another game, **"The African Dip."** Black men would sit on a bar, and every time a baseball hit the target, he would fall into a pool of water. [167] *Today, it's just called the Dunk Tank. This will not be the only time Blacks or other minorities will be put on display for White entertainment* **(See #40)**. Twenty-one years after conceiving the idea to gift something special for ending the enslavement of Black Americans, Frederic Bartholdi and Edouard de Laboulaye finally deliver the **Statue of Liberty** to America in 1886. But it's 21 years too late **(See #30)**. The statue is now seen as a welcoming symbol for newly arrived immigrants to America. *But at least now you know what Lady Liberty actually stands for and why she has a broken chain on her foot as she steps forward — towards freedom.* [168 169]

**38. 1890-1896.**

**"We came here to exclude the Negro. Nothing short of this will answer." - Mississippi Supreme Court Justice Solomon Calhoon, 1890.** Remember 41 years ago, when the Order of the Star-Spangled Banner established anti-everything behind fears of being greatly replaced **(See #24)**? And that time 25 years ago, when Andrew Johnson told the ex- Confederates to rebuild their governments after the Civil War **(See #30)**? And just 19 years after that when the 15th Amendment increased Black voter participation and Black politicians like Menard, Revels, and Rainey won seats in Congress **(See #33, #35)**? Well, to ensure Black voting and Black congressional representation would decrease, while also making sure the government was rebuilt to benefit themselves so they wouldn't be significantly replaced, **southern states legalized voter rights discrimination.** [170] [171] Now you must own property, pay poll taxes (literally pay money to vote), and be able to read.[172] If you can read, you also must be able to pass an unpassable test graded by a White registrant whose guidance and direction from their employer and the state is to fail you, no matter how well you do. You may also remember that owning land, buying property, and having enough self-sustaining and disposable income have been illegal and suppressed for Black Americans in the south since the Slave Codes of 1662 **(See #5, #6)**, the Negro Act of 1740 **(See #8, #45)**, the Dred Scott decision of 1857 **(See #25)**, and the Black Codes of 1865

**(See #31).** [173][174] *Translation: It is literally impossible for most Black people to register to vote.* They also create the **Grandfather Clause**. If your grandaddy could vote, then so could you, serving as a safety net for poor Whites who also fall under the "no land and can't read" category. [175] These anti-Black voting methods were so effective that Black men's voting percentage in Mississippi went from 90% to 6% in 1892. 1892 is also the same year Ida B. Wells **(See #28, #40, #42, #46)** writes her first article on White mob violence and lynching after her friend is lynched. Like the anger in 1866 **(See #32)**, the Memphis, Tennessee locals are so enraged they burn down her printing press and run her out of town. Two years later, the **United Daughters of the Confederacy (UDC)** is formed to protect and honor the Confederate struggle during and after the Civil War **(See #31, #44, #45)**. These descendants of Confederate veterans, and those who supported their cause, directed most of their efforts toward raising funds for Confederate monuments and Confederate named sites **(See #44, #97, #98)** and spearheading a new literary revolution **(See #45, #99)** by teaching the "correct" history of the Confederacy using Edward Pollard's "Lost Cause" writings **(See #31)**. Meanwhile, in New Orleans, **Homer Plessy** tries to end racial segregation by sitting down in the "Whites Only" carriage. He is arrested after refusing to get up and arguing that he is "7/8 White."

In court, he loses the 13th and 14th Amendment battle with Judge John Howard Ferguson. The Supreme Court backs Ferguson's verdict, proclaiming Blacks are **"separate, but equal" and "the act of physically separating people did not make them inferior."** As a result of the Supreme Court's decision, *Plessy v. Ferguson* sets a national precedent that allows the states to decide what "reasonable" is when it came to racial "equality." [176][177] *This is what states' rights would have looked like from 1861-1865.* The legalization and violent suppression of Black freedom in the south juxtaposed with the perception of the more liberal and blue-collar opportunities in the north inspire the **"Great Migration."** Thousands of southern Blacks pack up their things and leave the south for good **(See #42, #61, #76).** [178][179] As hundreds of thousands of Blacks move to the Midwest, all-White enclaves known as **Sundown** (*"Don't Let the Sun go down on you Nigger"*) **and Anna** (*Ain't No Niggers Allowed"*) **towns** begin expanding **(See #54).** [180][181] *These towns legally "ended" around the 1970s, but the systemic and suburban ideology of "No Black's allowed here" still exists today.* Back in D.C., W.E.B. Du Bois, now the first Black PhD graduate from Harvard, gives an address titled *"The Study of the Negro Problem"* and addresses the American Negro Academy on *"The Conservation of the Races,"* a call to defend Black culture and identity. These two works define his understanding of the race problem in America and lead to one of his most renowned works **(See #40).** [182]

**39. 1898.**

In February, the U.S.S. Maine blows up in Cuba, igniting the Spanish American War and Cuba's fight for independence from Spain. As a result, 2,500 Blacks join the fight for... freedom? **(See #9, #19, #28, #31, #44, #54, #58, #61, #84, #87, #100).** [183] Meanwhile, a couple of years after Downing invents and patents the mailbox **(See #37)**, another Black inventor, F.W. **Leslie,** successfully patents the envelope seal so your mail didn't fall out when you dropped it in that mailbox that a Black man also invented. *This seal eventually turns into that lickable envelope glue known as "gum Arabic."* Oh, and a quick side note while we are on inventions: **George Franklin Grant** will invent the golf tee one year later. *Thank him next time you're missing all those colorful golf holes at Top Golf.* By November, Blacks are fighting for someone elses freedom in Cuba and fighting for their lives in Wilmington, North Carolina. Fed up with the freedom and social and political progress of Black people in Wilmington, former Confederate Colonel Alfred Waddell rallies a massive crowd of 8,000 Klansmen, politicians, journalists, White supremacist speakers, and Red Shirts, a paramilitary arm of the Democrat Party, and they vow to put an end to "Negro Domination." He then announces **"White Man's Day."** He reads from the White Declaration of Independence: *"We, the undersigned citizens... do hereby declare that we will no longer be ruled and will NEVER again be ruled by men of African origin."* So riled up, the Red Shirts and others begin attacking every Black resident they see every single night.

They burn down the only Black-owned newspaper shop, and they force every Black leader to the nearest train station and send them out of town. Sixty people are killed, and the local government, including its Black political representatives, is replaced by Waddell-nominated White supremacists. *The Wilmington Massacre is the only successful government coup d'état in American history and the first of two ever. The second attempt comes 123 years later* (See #98). [184][185]

### 40. 1900-1904. Lift Every Voice And...

Despite her print shop being burned down, Ida B. Wells (See #28, #38, #42, #46) keeps writing and exposing the lies justifying lynching in her famous essay, *A Lynch Law in America.* [186] This is the same year **James Weldon Johnson (See #42, #44, #46)** writes **"Lift Every Voice and Sing,"** which becomes the official "Negro National Hymn." *Because the first "national" hymn was clearly written for someone else* (See #19, #51). [187][188] One year later, Theodore Roosevelt invites Booker T. Washington (See #25, #30, #37, #41, #43, #46) to dine with him at the White House. Like Lincoln needed Frederick Douglass (See #27, #29), Roosevelt leaned on Washington to discuss racial matters. [189] He is technically the first Black American formally invited to the House, which, as you can expect, causes an uproar among Whites, especially in the Jim Crow south. *Frederick Douglass popped up unannounced the first time but received the open-door policy afterward.* In 1903, Washington's ideological archnemesis,

W.E.B. Du Bois, publishes *The Souls of Black Folk*, a collection of philosophical essays on race, **the "veil" and "double consciousness,"** labor, and American African culture. [190][191] *The "veil" is a visual metaphor of the color line and a symbolic representation of how Blacks and Whites view the world and one another vastly different. The "double consciousness" is the internal conflict experienced by subordinate or colonized groups in oppressive societies and the sense of always looking at one's self through the eyes of others (i.e., their oppressors).* **Mary McLeod Bethune** opens the Daytona Literary and Industrial Training School for Negro Girls "with $1.50, faith in God, and five little girls." Today, the school is known as Bethune-Cookman College. And in St. Louis, the 1904 World Expo Fair is showcasing its first **"Human Zoo."** [192][193] Twenty million visitors come to see Hindu rope dancers, Filipino "head hunters," Chilean Kawesqar Indians, Arabian camel herders, Australian Aboriginals, and Congolese Pygmies, like **Ota Benga**, [194] cut stone tools or perform religious and food rituals, and war practices. *Indigenous humans were caged and placed on a timeline between apes and European White men. These zoos confirm that anything non-European can and will be considered property and entertainment.* The formerly enslaved **Nancy Green** is now a spokesperson for the R.T. Davis Milling Company. *The company is later known as Quaker Oats and PepsiCo.* Her second time working with the company, Green arrives at the Expo making an appearance as **"Aunt Jemima,"** (See #47, #97) a caricature rooted in the "mammy" stereotype (See #21). [195] Green sings old southern Confederate songs at the expo while making pancakes for White customers and forever cementing the Aunt Jemima character. [196]

**41. 1905-1906.**

"My object is to teach the north, the young north, what it has never known—the awful suffering of the White man during the dreadful Reconstruction period. I believe that Almighty God anointed the White men of the south by their suffering during that time… to demonstrate to the world that the White man must and shall be supreme." Author **Thomas Dixon**, a university classmate and friend to future president Woodrow Wilson **(See #43)**, publishes *The Clansmen*. [197] The novel sought to rebuke Harriet Beecher Stowe's book **(See #24)** and reimagined the Civil War and Reconstruction Era as an attack on the south. The novel also glorifies the return of the Ku Klux Klan **(See #43)** and honors their chivalrous gallantry to defend their Aryan birthright and protect White women from the savage lust of Black men. *This stereotype specifically and the White protectionist supremacy of White women will be super relevant throughout various tragedies in history* **(See #42, #47, #48, #52, #58, #61, #62, #83, #84)**. Watching all of this take place, W.E.B. Du Bois looks to directly challenge Booker T. Washington's integrationist approach and forms the **Niagara Movement** in hopes of developing a more militant movement against racial inequality. [198] Meanwhile in the Midwest, Native Americans announce the sale of their territorial lands in Oklahoma during the Land Rush of 1899. Wealthy Black businessmen

John the Baptist (J.B.) Stradford and O.W. Gurley [199]
take advantage and purchase more than 40 acres in the
"oil capital of the world" - Tulsa, Oklahoma. After
planning the creation of an all-Black community,
Gurley and Stradford subdivide the land into
commercial and residential lots - *only to be sold to
coloreds"* - build a hotel, grocery store, and boarding
house for traveling Black residents, and name the area
**Greenwood**. The town eventually grows into 35 blocks
of all-Black and all-prosperous banks, stores, jewelers,
barbershops, salons, restaurants, taverns, pool halls, the
iconic Williams Dreamland Theater, lawyer offices,
dentists, and home to "the most able Negro surgeon in
America," **Dr. A.C. Jackson**. Their schools were elite,
and their teachers were the highest paid in the
community. Their homes were all brick and furnished
by Louis Vuitton dining room sets, fine china, and
Steinway pianos. Booker T. Washington called the self-
sustaining Greenwood District **"Negro Wall Street of
America."** But everything changes when a scream is
heard in an elevator **(See #46)**.[200] After learning all the
hair secrets from  Black millionaire **Annie Turnbo
Malone's** Wonderful Hair Grower shop, **Sarah
Breedlove, now known as Madam C.J. Walker**, opens
her first hair business, Walker's Wonderful Hair
Grower, in Denver, Colorado. So successful, she
employs hundreds of women all over the nation and is
now on her way to becoming another one of the first
Black millionaires. *Allow me to drop another quick*

*reminder that money does not make you immune to racism and discrimination.* And on the east coast, the first Black fraternity, **Alpha Phi Alpha**, is being officially founded at Cornell University.

**42. 1908-1911.**

Two years after the first Black fraternity, the first Black sorority in the country, **Alpha Kappa Alpha**, is founded at Howard University. A few hours north, in New York, W.E.B. Du Bois **(See #52)**, Ida B. Wells **(See #28, #38, #40, #46)**, Mary White Ovington, and Moorfield Storey establish the **National Association for the Advancement of Colored People (NAACP)**. *Specifically because of the 41 things listed before this.* Initially, the NAACP's national leaders were White progressives like Ovington and Storey, but after World War I, Black male leadership increased with James Weldon Johnson **(See #41, #44, #46)** and **Walter White (See #46)** joining the ranks. *Walter White was a Black man born with blonde hair and blue eyes. Using this to his advantage, he went undercover to investigate more than 40 lynchings and eight race riots throughout the South on behalf of the NAACP. He will later become NAACP president.* Additionally, the entire organization is boosted by the efforts of the **National Association of Colored Women (NACW)**, led by Ida B. Wells, Juanita Jackson Mitchell, and **Ella Baker (See #63, #64, #67)**. [201] The group is successful in directly challenging racial inequalities and winning legal battles, as well as being a critical voice against lynching throughout the south. [202] [203] In 1910, while the NAACP focuses its investigative attention in the south, the Great Migration picks up speed out of the south. [204][205] **Jack Johnson** also defeats James Jeffries in the **"fight of the century"** to become the first Black heavyweight boxing champion. [206] His victory triggered a race riot and made him a target of racial discrimination and government charges for violating the **Mann Act,** also known as the "White-Slave Traffic Act of 1910." [207] This act forbids the transportation of White women across state lines for "immoral purposes," but really, he was charged because of his open relationships with White women. *The Mann Act, a legal form of White protectionist supremacy, was invoked repeatedly to punish Black men for their relationships with White women. Other Examples: Chuck Berry and Malcolm Little* **(See #57).** One year later, on January 5, 1911, 10 Black college students found **Kappa Alpha Psi** on the all-White, KKK-surrounded campus of Indiana University. It was the first Black fraternity founded at a predominantly White institution. *Xi Rho (DePauw University), Fall 05, Deuce Klub. Handshake, handshake, handshake. Quick shout out to the Nupes. Of course I had to.* Eleven months later, **Omega Psi Phi** is founded at Howard, followed by **Delta Sigma Theta** two years later. *These are the roots of Black collegiate men and women building a brotherhood and sisterhood of achievement, success, and legacy.*

**43. 1914-1915. The Birth of a Nation.**

A third fraternity, **Phi Beta Sigma**, is founded just one month before Rosa Parks is born in Tuskegee, Alabama **(See #53),** and two months before Harriet "Moses"

Tubman passes away in Auburn, New York **(See #20, #23, #24, #27)**. [208] *The woman courageously went back into slavery for 11 years, in the era of the Fugitive Slave Acts and kidnapping, not once, not twice, but 19 times to rescue 70 more enslaved persons and became the first female military intelligence analyst and the first woman to lead a military expedition for the northern Union army during the Civil War and still found the time to fight for women's rights. Forever Legendary.* One year later, Booker T. Washington passes away **(See #25, #30, #37, #40, #41, #46)**. At the time of his death, Tuskegee University grew into 100 well-equipped buildings, 1,500 Black students, and 200 teachers teaching 38 trades and professions and an endowment of two million dollars ($53 million today). *Washington, like Frederick Douglass, believed that Black Americans would gradually be accepted by Whites and gain full participation in society so long as they played their part by providing needed skills and acted as "responsible, reliable American citizens." Because of these ideas, he was at great odds with W.E.B. Du Bois,* [209] *who believed in Black militancy and self-determination, like Martin Delany* **(See #24)**. *Du Bois also believed that Washington was much too accommodating to White interests – the "Uncle Tom" debate* **(See #24)**. *They were the Martin and Malcolm of their time* **(See #69)**. *Nevertheless, they were two men who aspired to see Blackness at its greatness, and Washington's impact across history had lasting effects.* Forty-nine years after the First Order **(See #24, #32), the Second Order, or "The Rebirth" of the Ku Klux Klan**, is inspired by D.W. Griffith's film,

*Birth of a Nation* **(See #44, #94)**. [210] This three-hour revisionist cultural phenomena is based on Thomas Dixon's *The Clansmen* novel **(See #41)** and becomes America's first feature-length motion picture and first box office smash. [211] [212] *It's also noted as "the most controversial film ever made in the United States."* Confederate-loving, KKK-praising President Woodrow Wilson **(See #45, #46, #51, #96)** hosts a screening of the movie in the East Room as a favor to his old college friend Dixon. This is the very first film ever featured at the White House. "It's like writing history with lightning. My only regret is that it is all so terribly true." *That is an actual quote made by Woodrow Wilson.* [213] While the NAACP protests every premier, the film ignites riots across the country and inspires mobs of White crowds to attack Blacks across numerous cities. In July, six months after the film's release, Jewish factory superintendent Leo Frank is found guilty of the alleged rape and murder of one of his employees in Atlanta, Georgia, 13-year-old Mary Phagan. On August 16, 25 White men, inspired by the film and identifying themselves as The Knights of Mary Phagan, caravan to Milledgeville Prison, take Frank from his cell, drive him back to Marietta, Phagan's hometown, and hang him from an oak tree. The next morning, nearly three thousand people gather to view and abuse Frank's hanging body until authorities take it away. [214] Three months after the murder of Frank and after watching *Birth of a Nation*, Georgia preacher William J. Simmons obtains copies of

Nathan Forrest's First Order bylaws **(See #32)** and begins writing his own revised version. On Thanksgiving night, Simmons and the Mary Phagan Knights climb Stone Mountain, burn a cross and officially inaugurate the **Second Order of the Ku Klux Klan.** [215][216] This Thomas Dixon-D.W. Griffith-inspired new Klan sees itself as the vengeful vanguard for the south and White supremacy. At the same time, lynchings, fear, voter suppression, and murder becomes the new state-sanctioned norm throughout the entire south, supported by police, judges, Woodrow Wilson, and the Supreme Court. [217][218]

**44. 1916-1917. Up, You Mighty Race!**

Ohioan **Garrett Morgan (See #46)** invents the Morgan Smoke Hood for firefighters. He knows White fire chiefs won't buy from a Black man, so he pays a White actor to sell it for him. While the actor pitches sales, Morgan disguises himself as "Big Chief Mason," the actor's Native American sidekick, who creates a fire inside the tent and stays inside for 20 minutes only to emerge unharmed. So impressed, firefighters all over the nation put in their orders, including the U.S. military, which makes it a standard issue for soldiers during WW1. [219] This is also the same year Jamaican-born activist **Marcus Garvey (See #45, #48, #49, #62, #71)** moves to Harlem to study the American Black population. Because the U.S. intended to deny Blacks integrated equal rights, he establishes the **Universal Negro Improvement Association (UNIA).**

*"Up, you mighty race!"* The UNIA channels their inner Martin Delany **(See #24)** and advocates for a "separate, but equal" status and the establishment of independent Black states around the country. [220][221] The Garvey movement inspires thousands of Blacks, including **Elijah Robert Poole (See #51), Earl Little, and Louise Langdon (See #48, #49, #51)**. The same year, President Wilson plays guest of honor at the $27^{th}$ reunion of the United Confederate Veterans and United Daughters of the Confederacy **(See #38, #44, #97, #98)**. Thousands came to hear Wilson speak, and his address fully embraces the "Lost Cause" **(See #31, #45, #51)**, recalling how **"heroic things were done on both sides."** *Sounds eerily familiar to what another president will say about the "neo" version of this crowd in exactly 100 years* **(See #96)**. One month later, Wilson directs Army General Joseph Kuhn to assign names to the country's first new Army bases. He does. And all names honor Confederate generals **(See #54, #98)**: Camp Beauregard in Louisiana is named after Pierre G.T. Beauregard. Fort Gordon in Georgia after John Brown Gordon, the head of the Ku Klux Klan in Georgia. Fort Bragg in North Carolina, after Braxton Bragg. Fort Benning in Georgia after Henry Lewis Benning, slavery enthusiast. Fort Lee in Virginia after Robert E. Lee. [222] Meanwhile, up north, James Weldon Johnson **(See #41, #42, #46)** is organizing the very first civil rights protest, **The Silent Drum**. The June march is accompanied only by the sound of drums as 10,000 Black men and women march through the

the streets of Manhattan. Four months later, **Fannie Lou Hamer (See #39, #59)** is born into a Mississippi sharecropping family. Although ongoing since 1914, this is the first year the U.S. enters World War I. To rile up the troops, President Wilson signs an executive order making Francis Scott Key's "Star-Spangled Banner" the national anthem for the military **(See #19, #51)**. [223] Some 370,000 Blacks, including the Harlem Hellfighters, stand at attention while the anthem is played for the first time after joining the fight for... freedom? **(See #9, #19, #28, #31, #39, #54, #58, #61, #84, #87, #100)**. [224][225][226][227][228]

## 45. 1919. The Red Summer.

After four years, WWI ends. That same year, the Birth of a Nation, Lost Cause president wins a Nobel Peace Prize for his efforts to ensure world peace. But there is no peace at home. Hundreds of Black men and veterans are killed by White supremacists in an event that comes to be known as the **"Red Summer of 1919."** [229] The same year, the NAACP publishes 30 Years of Lynching in the United States: 1898-1918, a pamphlet that details the lynching of 83 Black people, many of them soldiers returning home from the war. In response to the tragedies, the first Black filmmaker **Oscar Micheaux** writes what will soon be the critically acclaimed silent film, *Within Our Gates*. The film focuses on race relations in the 1920s, Jim Crow, the rise of the KKK, the Great Migration, and the emergence of the **"New Negro."**

Outside of the movie theaters, more Negro Act **(See #8, #38)** type actions are enforced, signaled by the new **Racially Restrictive Covenant laws (See #49, #59, #88)**. White property owners are now banning all house sales to Black buyers. *Thus enforcing and legalizing that age-old idea of Blacks not being allowed to own property* **(See #6, #8, #25, #31)** *which is officially established into federal law 15 years later* **(See #52)**. [230] [231] [232] [233] With the full backing of President Wilson, the United Daughters of the Confederacy continue teaching the "Lost Cause" **(See #31, #44, #51)** and pledge to change history books with the **"Textbook Revolution."** They ban all Northern, pro-Union, Lincoln-focused history books and any book mentioning the south fighting for slavery and replace them with words and ideas like "northern aggressor" and "states' rights." [234] And as history was being rewritten, 24-year-old John Edgar Hoover **(See #48)** is promoted to head of the Bureau of Investigation's new General Intelligence Division, also known as the Radical Division **(See #62)**. His goal: monitor, disrupt, arrest, and deport all domestic radicals, which currently include Communists, Italian anarchists, and Black nationalist advocates like Marcus Garvey **(See #44)**.

**46. 1920-1922. A New Negro and the Tulsa Massacre.**

**Zeta Phi Beta** is the third sorority founded at Howard in the same year that **Henrietta Lacks** is born in Roanoke, Virginia. She will become immortal in 31 years. 1920 is also **the Golden Era of Black and the era of the New Negro.**

The moniker originates with the work of **Alain Locke** and represents Black self-determination, pride, and courageous defiance. The era also includes the **Harlem Renaissance** becomes a geographic metaphor for the rising influence of the Black narrative, invention, creativity, and culture. [235] [236] **The Negro National Baseball League** is founded. **James Van Der Zee** begins his career as a photojournalist and will become the most iconic photographer of Black life. **Bessie Coleman** becomes the first Black woman to obtain a pilot's license and fly a plane. **Aaron Douglas** becomes the Father of Black American art. **Claude McKay and Langston Hughes** capture Black life and struggle with poetic and literary precision. And **Louie Armstrong, Duke Ellington, and Bessie Smith** provide the soundtrack to it all. To top things off, President Woodrow Wilson finally passes the **19th Amendment.** After 42 years of a very long sexist, racist, and still male-dominated battle, women now have the right to vote. *Something which angered many White women suffragists during their fight because Black men got the right to vote (on paper) before they did.* But now, women everywhere can legally cast a ballot, except southern Black women. Because unfortunately, while the Black renaissance is sweeping through the north, the Black vote, male and female, is being eroded down south thanks to poll taxes, grandfather clauses, literacy tests, ownership laws, and voter intimidation and violence **(See #38)**. Land and communities are being destroyed as well, highlighted by the events in Tulsa, Oklahoma in 1921.

17-year-old Sarah Page screams after 19-year-old Dick Rowland trips and grabs onto her while walking into the elevator where she is working **(See #41)**. The department store clerk hears the scream, sees Dick run out of the store, and calls the police. Rowland knew when a White woman screams, a Black man is always found guilty. By the afternoon, the local White newspaper, The Tulsa Tribune, publishes the headlines *"Nab Negro for Attacking Girl in Elevator"* on the front page. While the police arrest Rowland and charge him with assaulting a White woman, rumors quickly get around the White side of the railroad tracks that Dick raped young Sarah. Angered and full of revenge, hundreds of armed White men arrive at the downtown courthouse looking to lynch Rowland. *White protectionist supremacy.* But they are met by a group of armed Black veterans, which sparks a shootout on Main Street. The violence eventually spills over into the unsuspecting Greenwood District, and things turn for the worse. Thirty-five blocks of Black homes and businesses are bombed, burned, and looted. White men in crop planes drop dynamite and kerosene bombs over Greenwood, making it the first time ever an American city had been under aerial attack. In three days, some 800 are injured and 300 are dead, including Dr. A.C. Jackson. The $80,000 Mt. Zion Baptist Church is burned to the ground. 10,000 Blacks are displaced. Countless victims are unconfirmed and unaccounted and believed to have been thrown in a local river or buried in unmarked mass graves. Close to 7,000 Black residents are arrested by the Oklahoma National Guard, Tulsa Police, and White deputized locals, placed in internment camps for weeks, and forced to clean up the damage on the White side of town. Those who stayed were left to rebuild their lives, while others who dodged murder or arrests, like J.B. Stradford and O.W. Gurley, made the difficult decision to leave Greenwood for good. Gurley lost nearly $158,000 ($2.3 million today), moved to Los Angeles, and died 13 years later with nothing. In total, approximately two million dollars in property damages was destroyed ($27 million today). [237] *The Tulsa Race Riot is documented as the largest racial massacre in American history. But this story remains buried for 80 more years* **(See #87)**. That same year, James Weldon Johnson **(See #41, #42, #44)**, Ida B. Wells **(See #28, #38, #40, #42)**, Walter White **(See #42)**, and others work to get the **Dyer Anti-Lynching Bill** passed. A first of its kind, the bill declares lynching and mob violence a violation of the 14th Amendment **(See #33)**. The bill passes in the House of Reps, 231-119, but is blocked in the Senate by southern Democrats. *And 100 years later...***(See #97, #99, #100)**. Like Kappa Alpha Psi **(See #42)**, **Sigma Gamma Rho** sorority will be founded at the predominantly White institution of Butler University in Indianapolis, Indiana. And six years after selling the firefighter and military smoke hood **(See #44)**, Garrett Morgan comes up with his second major invention after witnessing a disastrous accident between an automobile and a horse carriage at an intersection. The yellow caution signal and the three signal traffic light. One year later, Morgan patents his invention and eventually sells the idea to General Electric for $40,000 ($500,000 today).

**47. 1923.**

Nancy Green **(See #40)** is hit by a vehicle in Chicago and killed. Although signing a lifetime contract with R.T. Davis Milling Company, neither she nor her family ever receive any revenue for her years as "Aunt Jemima." [238] [239] Green is immediately replaced, and the pancake-making mammy caricature lives on, acted out by at least nine other Black women over the course of 40 years. No one will ever know of Nancy Green, the world's first living trademark, until she is brought back up 97 years later **(See #97)**. Down south, the Klan is making sure what happened in the Greenwood District of Tulsa also happens to the all-Black community of **Rosewood, Florida**. Twenty-two year old Francis Taylor wakes up the all-White town of Sumner with a scream. *Yes, another scream.* Her neighbors rush to her home and find her covered in bruises. Francis claims a Black man entered the house and assaulted her. Rumor quickly spreads that she was raped and robbed, despite telling the sheriff she was not. More than 500 Klansmen travel to Rosewood - Sumner's all-Black neighbor. *White protectionist supremacy.* Homes, stores, and churches are burned down. At least eight Black residents are killed. Many flee to the swamps to hide, and those who survive never return. A judge hears over 30 eyewitness testimonies and concludes he cannot find enough evidence to convict anyone. And Francis? All a lie. She was beaten by her lover, John Bradley, who had come by to see her while her husband was at work. Instead of telling her husband she was cheating, she blamed a Black man and burned down an entire Black town to hide her infidelities. [240]

## 48. 1925. The Federal Bureau of Investigation.

For three hours, 30,000 unmasked, fully robed Klansmen march on Washington, D.C. With Greenwood and Rosewood adding proof to the UNIA's agenda of racial separation **(See #44)**, Garvey meets with the Klan to compromise and collectively push his goal: Separate, but equal. There are more than 5,000 Blacks in the organization and countless supporters, but this meeting significantly reduces his appeal among Black Americans. Five years after leading the Radical Division, J. Edgar Hoover is promoted again. This time as the new director of the **Federal Bureau of Investigation (FBI) (See #45, #48, #49, #58, #62, #68, #75, #77, #79, #100)**. *In about 32 years, he will begin to singlehandedly dismantle Black leaders and Black movements* **(See #62)**. UNIA members Earl Little and Louise Langdon **(See #44)** are now married and move to Nebraska, hoping for a better life. And almost exactly one year after Hoover takes over the FBI, **Malcolm Little**, their fourth child of seven, is born in Omaha on May 19 **(See #51, #57, #58)**.

**49. 1926-1928.**

**Dr. Carter G. Woodson**, the second Black Harvard graduate after W.E.B. Du Bois, announces that **"Negro History Week" (See #75, #79)** will coincide with the birthdays of Abraham Lincoln (February 12) and Frederick Douglass (February 14). The event will solidify the New Negro and commemorate Black cultural and historical accomplishments. [241] *This commemoration will expand significantly in the next 43 years* **(See #75)**. After eight years of being monitored by Hoover, Marcus Garvey is arrested and deported back to Jamaica for mail fraud and illegally selling stock shares - but really it was for his Black nationalist advocacy. He is never seen in the states again. *His time was short-lived, but his legacy of Black Pride will set a foundation for future generations* **(See #71)**. The Little family leaves Omaha and moves to Lansing, Michigan. They settle in a White neighborhood but soon face eviction notices due to Racially Restrictive Covenant laws **(See #45, #59, #88)**. *These were the same ones enacted in 1919. How many years of denied Black ownership will we get?* Defiant not to move, the house is burned to the ground, and they are forced to move to East Lansing.

**50. 1929. A Greater Depression.**

**Michael Lewis King** is born in Atlanta, Georgia, on January 15. This is the same year North Carolina passes the **Eugenics Law** and legalizes the sterilization of Black and minority women. [242] *This becomes the first 40-year experiment on Black people (1929-1974).*

*Things they do to you when you are still not considered human. This is also one of many reasons Blacks do not trust hospitals or science* **(See #6, #51, #57, #59, #74, #79, #97)**. Wall Street and the stock market crashes, losing 90% of their value, and the Great Depression begins. The economy shrinks by 50% and 33% of banks fail. Unemployment rises to 25% and homelessness increases. Housing prices plummet, foreclosures rise and (Herbert) "Hooverville" shantytowns spring up everywhere. [243][244][245] *The Great Depression will last for the next 10 years and will also reveal who gets help and who does not - especially with one of the most prominent ways of earning wealth, housing* **(See #52)**.

**51. 1930-1932.**

Salesman **Wallace Fard Muhammad** begins teaching Blacks about Islam and Black nationalism in Detroit, Michigan. These teachings evolve into the establishment of **Temple No. 1 of the Nation of Islam (NOI) (See #58, #66, #69, #70)**. *Somewhat ironically, maybe intentional, but this happened on July 4.* The nationalist group focuses on improving Black lives by achieving independence through separation from the rest of society. Tired of the Jim Crow South, **Elijah Poole (See #44)** joins the Great Migration, and moves to Detroit. *"I seen enough of the White man's brutality to last me 26,000 years." - Elijah Poole.* He ends up meeting Wallace, and after seeing similarities to Garvey's UNIA, he joins the NOI and changes his name to **Elijah Muhammad (See #52, #58, #66, #68)**.

Another former UNIA member Earl Little is one hour away preaching in Lansing until he is run over and killed by the racist terrorist group known as the "Black Legion" one year later. His Black Pride messages likely being the reason. Months later, Malcolm's widowed mother, Louisa Little, suffers a nervous breakdown and is institutionalized at Kalamazoo State Hospital. A young Malcolm is left parentless. Fifteen years after Woodrow Wilson named it the military song **(See #44)**, Congress passes legislation on March 3, 1931, making Francis Scott Key's 117-year-old poem **(See #19)** the National Anthem of the United States. [246][247] *Yet another reason why James Weldon Johnson wrote the Negro version* **(See #41)**. *This fact will be relevant again in 85 years* **(See #94)**. Twenty-two days later, nine young Black teenagers (ages 13-20) are accused of raping two White women in Scottsboro, Alabama. Behind false claims, the **"Scottsboro Boys"** are sentenced to death by an all-White jury **(See #44, #46, #53, #57, #58, #61, #67)**, shocking the nation. In a rather unexpected twists of events, the two White girls testify that they were never raped and they join in the fight to release the boys. [248] *This case pushes a major Supreme Court decision in four years* **(See #53)**. In 1932, three years after North Carolina passes the Eugenics Law **(See #50)**, the U.S. Public Health Service (USPHS) and the **Center for Disease Control (CDC)** initiates the second 40-year experiment on Black people in Macon County, Alabama: **The Tuskegee Syphilis Study of Untreated Syphilis in the Negro Male** whereby 600 Black men are told they will be tested for "bad blood." Yet, 399 of those men were never told they had syphilis. The 201 who did not have the disease were never told they were the control group. They were subjects for observation for 40 years without their consent, never told of their issues, and never given a treatment **(See #57)**. [249] [250] *Things they do to you when what? You ain't considered human. Another reason Blacks do not trust hospitals or science* **(See #6, #50, #57, #59, #74, #79, #97)**. With the military bases out of the way, North Carolina becomes one of the first states to begin naming schools after Confederate leaders, thanks to the "Lost Cause" **(See #31, #44, #45)**. And after all that's happened, six-year-old Malcolm Little's views on how Black people are treated in America begin to take shape **(See #48, #57, #58)**. *O'er the land of the free and the home of the brave ...*

## 52. 1933-1934.

After being inspired by the famed German professor and priest of the same name Michael Lewis King Sr. changes his and his four year old son's name to Martin Luther King Sr. and Jr. during a trip to Berlin, Germany **(See #57)**. Dr. Carter G. Woodson **(See #49, #75)** publishes the *Mis-education of the Negro*, detailing everything wrong about the American education system and how it "educates" Black students. *Still very relevant to all the arguments today* **(See #99)**. [251] Founder Wallace Muhammad disappears, and Elijah Muhammad takes over the NOI, relocating the HQ (Temple No. 2) to Chicago, Illinois. [252] The group has gained a significant number of followers due to its anti-White rhetoric and message of self-determination.

However, the NOI's Black critics view the movement as detrimental to the more gradual integrationist movement. After 24 years, W.E.B. Du Bois leaves the NAACP **(See #42)**. His interest in Black nationalism and radical appeal to fight racism is no longer aligned with the organization's goals. New president, Franklin D. Roosevelt, enacts his New Deal policies in an effort to reinflate the economy and restrain the banking industry after the Wall Street crash of 1929 **(See #50)**. He also establishes the **U.S. Department of Housing and Urban Development (HUD) and the Federal Housing Administration (FHA)**. The goal of the new organizations is to improve housing standards and assist (White) families with better home financing after the Great Depression **(See #50)**. [253] While White families buy homes with FHA assistance, Black families receive redlined property, high-interest rates, and housing discrimination in mortgage lending. They are also forced into public housing projects like Atlanta's Techwood Homes, the first to open in Georgia for the Black and houseless. [254 255 256 257 258]

**53. 1935-1937.**

The U.S. Supreme Court rules in Norris v. Alabama that a defendant has the right to a trial by a jury of their peers. *Because of too many all-White juries, Guilty for Blacks and Not Guilty for Whites trials* **(See #44, #46, #51, #57, #58, #61, #67)**. The court also discovers Black people have never been made jurors, and deliberate exclusion based on race was deemed unconstitutional.

This major court decision helps to overturn the Scottsboro Boys' "guilty" death sentence conviction **(See #51)**. Still, in the courtrooms, President Franklin D. Roosevelt appoints the first federal Black judge, **William H. Hastie**. Across the water in Berlin, Germany, **Jesse Owens and Ralph Metcalf (See #77)** are ruining Adolph Hitler's plans to prove "Aryan Supremacy" by winning multiple Olympic medals. Jesse, alone, wins four gold medals. But back home, White supremacy is winning gold and Black Americans are still in last place because of housing discrimination. By 1937, more and more FHA-approved White communities are developed, and "White flight" is being encouraged **(See #59)**. [259][260] In response, **Victor Hugo Green** creates *The Negro Motorized Green Book (commonly known as The Green Book)* for Black travelers to avoid the racist, segregated, unsafe, and unwelcoming sundown and communities **(See #38)**. [261]

[262] *The same towns inspired the 2018 film, The Green Book and were a key plot point in the Matt Ruff novel and HBO series, Lovecraft Country.* Living cramped in low-income project homes, Black Americans feel a bit of collective success when **Joe Louis** defeats James Braddock and becomes the second Black heavyweight champ after Jack Johnson's victory 27 years prior **(See #42)**. *The minor cultural victories provide the most temporary relief to real-world helpless struggles.*

**54. 1939-1941.**

The U.S. enters **World War II** two years after the war begins and after the attack on Pearl Harbor, Hawaii. Five more bases open—and five more Confederate Generals are honored **(See #44, #98)**: Fort Polk in Louisiana is named after Leonidas Polk, an enslaver. Fort Rucker in Alabama after Edmund W. Rucker. Fort A.P. Hill in Virginia after Ambrose Powell Hill. Fort Pickett in Virginia after George E. Pickett. And Fort Hood in Texas after John Bell Hood. Over one million Blacks are drafted and train at those Confederate named bases, including **Benjamin Oliver Davis**, the first Black general of the first Black air squadron known as the **Tuskegee Airmen** and the **761st Black Panther Tank Battalion**. And Black soldiers are still fighting for… freedom? **(See #9, #19, #28, #31, #39, #44, #58, #61, #84, #87, #100)**. Lieutenant **Jack Roosevelt Robinson** is court-martialed from the military after refusing to move to the back of a segregated military bus at Ft. Hood, Texas. *This same defiance will come into historical effect in six more years* **(See #57)**. In D.C., **Ann Pauline "Pauli" Murray (See #55, #60, #62, #71)** is the only woman in her class at Howard University Law School. Realizing the discriminatory biases against race and women, she coins the term **"Jane Crow."** [263] Murray's newly-labeled theories ties directly to **Hattie McDaniel** winning the Academy Award for her portrayal as a mammy stereotype in *Gone with The Wind*. Despite the problematic role, she is the first Black American,

male or female, to receive the award. Three years after
Judge Hastie **(See #53)**, **Jane M. Bolin** is appointed as
the first Black female judge in the United States. She is
also the first Black woman to graduate Yale Law. And
**Richard Wright** pens his *Native Son* novel. It becomes
the first bestselling novel by a Black American author.

**55. 1942-1943.**

While the war goes on overseas, a group of interracial
students back stateside in Chicago establish the
**Congress of Racial Equality (CORE) (See #57, #62,
#66)** to coordinate nonviolent direct action, such as sit-
ins and boycotts, in the fight for civil rights in America.
[264] *They will advise the young Dr. King and be heavily
involved in planning many major protest movements in a
few years.* Rising lawyer **Thurgood Marshall (See #60,
#73, #99)** takes his "most important case" to the
Supreme Court, *Smith v. Allwright* **(See #57, #73, #97,
#99)**. Marshall argues that Texas's democratic primary
system allows Whites to dominate politics structurally
and prohibits Blacks from voting, violating the 14$^{th}$ and
15$^{th}$ Amendments **(See #35)**. *Sounds presently familiar.*
"The United States is a constitutional democracy. Its
organic law grants to all citizens a right to participate in
the choice of elected officials without restriction by
any state because of race." - The Supreme Court. *Oh Em
Gee! The highest court in the land finally sides in favor of
Black folks.* This law helps push the Civil Rights
Movement forward, and significantly increases Black
voter registration numbers from close to 800,000 in 1948
to well over one million by 1952.

At the same time, Pauli Murray **(See #54, #60, #62)** is debating with her Howard Law classmates that the 14th Amendment **(See #33, #46, #60, #62)** should be used to overturn *Plessy v. Ferguson* **(See #38)**. Alone in her theory, she writes an essay proposing how the amendment could be used just for that purpose. She then bets her professor, Spottswood Robinson, $10 that Jim Crow will end within 25 years. He keeps the essay just in case, quietly believing that it just may come in handy for some grand moment one day **(See #60)**.

### 56. 1945. A Dollar's Worth.

After the war ends, Black vets come home to nothing except violence - cue the Red Summer of WW1 **(See #45)**. **No Government Issued (GI) Bills. No bank loans. No Veterans Affairs (VA) housing privileges.** *We are 80 years removed from slavery and there is still no guaranteed income, housing, wealth, or assistance equal to that of White Americans for Blacks.* [265] [266] [267] Over 95% of those benefits went to White soldiers who were offered a FHA-funded, family-sized home in a brand-spanking-new neighborhood for a down payment of $1.00. [268] [269]

### 57. 1946-1947. A Soldier's Story.

WWII veteran **Isaac Woodard** has just returned from the war and is headed home. Still in uniform, he travels by Greyhound until he is taken off the bus by South Carolina police. The bus driver called the police on him for causing a "disturbance." He had only asked to use the restroom. They beat him with nightsticks in an alley until he goes blind and suffers partial amnesia. The next morning, he is found guilty of disorderly conduct and fined $50. After a sham trial, the officers plead "self-defense" and are acquitted in 30 minutes by an all-White jury **(See #44, #46, #51, #53, #58, #61, #67). "Not Guilty."** Another veteran, **Maceo Snipes**, comes back home to Taylor County, Georgia, to vote in the Georgia Democratic Primary. He knows it's dangerous, but he also knows Thurgood Marshall and the Supreme Court just paved the way with *Smith v. Allwright* **(See #55)**. He is the only Black person in town to vote. Two days later, four members of the Klan drive to the Snipes family sharecropping farm and shoot him. Bloodied and dying, Maceo and his mother walk three miles before finding a ride to the nearest hospital. After waiting six hours in the lobby, the doctor tells Miss Snipes her son needs a blood transfusion, but the hospital does not carry any **"Black blood."** Snipes dies two days later. *Another reason Blacks do not trust hospitals or science* **(See #6, #50, #59, #74, #79, #97)**. The Klan members who killed Snipes claims he pulled a knife out. It was "self-defense." The court and the all-White jury agree. **"Not Guilty."** *We are just getting started, but this "self-defense" and "not guilty" thing has been going on for a very long time.* The bravery and murder of Maceo Snipes angers and inspires a young 17-year-old Morehouse College student named **Martin Luther King Jr.** to act and figure out his place in the world **(See #60)**. On the opposite end, 20-year-old **Malcolm Little**, now known as "Detroit Red," is on his way to Charlestown State Prison in Massachusetts after being sentenced to eight to ten years for grand larceny, breaking and entering, and firearms possession. His harsh sentence was really because he was dating a White woman. *The Jack Johnson-Chuck Berry-Mann Act effect* **(See #42)**. And that same stubborn lieutenant who was kicked out of the military two years ago for not moving to the back of the bus **(See #54)** has just now left a meeting with Branch Rickey, president and general manager of the Brooklyn Dodgers. Jackie Robinson accepts a contract deal to not only play for the Dodgers but to desegregate Major League Baseball. Amidst extreme racism and discrimination, he will still go on to win Rookie of the Year. *Butterfly Effect Moment: If Robinson never gets discharged, he goes on to lead the 761st Tank Battalion against the Nazis in France. If that happens, what happens to him? And to baseball? Who desegregates its then?* Back in the Jim Crow south, CORE **(See #55)** is organizing the Journey of Reconciliation. The nonviolent protest will be a multi-state integrated bus ride through the south to test the reality of the transportation segregation laws. *This is a precursor to another major protest in 20 years* **(See #66)**. This is also the first year penicillin has been confirmed as the drug to treat syphilis. The U.S. government sponsors several public health programs all over the nation to get rid of the disease except in Macon County, Alabama, where the CDC is in its 15$^{th}$ year of the Tuskegee Study **(See #51)**. With new Black organizations and new charges towards Black independence, justice, and equality, America is on the verge of becoming very uncivil.

\*\*\*\*\*

# (UN)CIVIL

# CHAPTER III:
# 1948-1970

# Civil Rights in Uncivil Times

*When Chief Justice William O. Douglas traveled to India, the first question the Indian press asked him was, "Why does America tolerate the lynching of Negroes?" Douglas could give no response, justification, or reason to the Indian media. But in his absence of explanation emerged a surge of Black voices and a diversity of Black leaders dedicated to answering for themselves.*

*This was 1950.*

*Outwardly, middle-class America is enjoying the economic fruits of post-World War II. Television, pristine suburbs, and rock-n-roll culture all signal the "Golden Era of American Capitalism." All is well for America — well, White America. Glitz and glamour on its surface, but the mirror America chooses to see itself within is getting ready to shatter. While the country is scrambling with the Cold War against Russia* and the fear of the spread of Communism throughout the nation, the rest of the world mocks "American democracy" rhetoric against the backdrop of American reality. "And you are lynching Negroes!" they yell.

Backed into a corner and facing extermination, the Black Americans, tired of being tired, continues to fight for their life, limb, and souls with the unexplainable courage to face America head-on. With scathing literary critique, Bible-driven nonviolent marches, boycotts, and sit-ins or fearlessly armed in self-defense, peeking out of windows with automatic rifles aimed toward the face of American oppression, violence, inequality, and betrayal. The time for being passive is gone.

The Black children who grew up watching and hearing stories about the New Negro have finally grown up determined to decide life for themselves. Singing the chords of the Negro National Hymn in unison, the seeds planted by Marcus Garvey, Ida B. Wells, Booker T. Washington, and W.E.B. Du Bois finally begin to bloom into beautiful Black roses. As this cultural defiance begins to fester beneath the dirt roads of the south and the concrete streets of the north, chants of "civil rights" and "self-determination" emerge like an unrelenting tidal wave.

Some years after India questioned William Douglas, Chief Justice Earl Warren shared his concern for America in a speech to the American Bar Association. "Our American system, like all others, is on trial both at home and abroad." And the trial was just about to begin.

**This is the Uncivil Era.**

## 58. 1948-1950.

Malcolm Little **(See #57)** begins studying Islam after writing to Elijah Muhammad **(See #51, #52)**, who is also in prison in Michigan for sedition and violation of WWII draft laws. Once released from prison, Malcolm moves to Detroit and joins Temple No. 1 and the Nation of Islam **(See #51)**. Soon after, he rejects his surname "Little" and is forever known as **Malcolm X (See #60, #63, #66, #68, #69, #70, #71, #100)**. Reminiscent of the Scottsboro Boys **(See #51)**, the **Groveland Four (See #96)** make headlines the next year. Four Black men in Lake County, Florida are falsely accused of raping 17-year-old Norma Padgett and assaulting her husband. A manhunt ensues, and three of the men are captured. The police sheriff kills the fourth a week later. The remaining three are beaten and tortured into a false confession. News spreads around the town and a mob of more than 1,000 White men demands the men be released to them for lynching. The sheriff lies to the mob and says they are in the state prison, so the mob takes their vengeance against the Groveland Black community, shooting residents and setting homes on fire. *White protectionist supremacy – the bold confidence that you could do whatever you wanted, and you knew you would get away with it. There are no courtrooms, and if you did step foot in front of a judge, you were judged by a jury of like-minded, racially equal peers and freed within the hour.* Florida NAACP official **Harry T. Moore** takes the case to defend the Groveland men, but it doesn't matter.

An all-White jury **(See #44, #46, #51, #53, #57, #61, #67)** sentences one to life in prison, and two are given the death sentence. [270] [271] [272] Months later, Moore and his wife are assassinated by a bomb placed under their home. Hoover's FBI investigates the murder, but no one is ever convicted. Overseas, the Korean War begins (1950-1953). It took 185 years, but after President Harry S. Truman signs Executive Order 9981, every military branch is now officially desegregated for the first time ever. *Ever, ever? Yeah, ever, ever. Since the American Revolution ever* **(See #9)**. [273] Around 600,000 Blacks join the fight for... freedom? **(See #9, #19, #28, #31, #39, #44, #54, #61, #84, #87, #100)**. Speaking of war, **Ralph Bunche** wins the 1950 Nobel Peace Prize for mediating a "peace" pause during the Arab-Israeli war. He is the first Black American to win the award. *Which is a huge family win and a good reason to be first, considering his great, great, great, keep going, great grandfather was John Punch. Another very different kind of first 310 years ago* **(See #3)**.

**59. 1951-1953.**

**Ralph Ellison** publishes *Invisible Man* and **James Baldwin** publishes his first book, *Go Tell It on the Mountain*. Ten months after being diagnosed with cervical cancer, **Henrietta Lacks (See #46)** passes away at Johns Hopkins Hospital. Prior to her death, doctors removed a sample of her cells and studied them without her consent or knowledge. The cells were called **"HeLa"** and were so unique that they were used in other research studying the effects of toxins, drugs, hormones, viruses, and the polio vaccine development.

*Another reason Blacks do not trust hospitals or science* **(See #50, #51, #57, #74, #79, #97)**. Meanwhile, the Federal Housing Authority prioritizes White homeownership and encourages White flight and purchasing homes outside of the city center **(See #52, #53, #56)**. This is the creation of the suburbs. [274] [275] [276] As the post-WW2 nation continues its rise to becoming more industrial, the south is still the south and drowning in a cesspool of discrimination and racist policies. And in the north and midwest, racism is showing its ugliness as more Blacks continue to pour in from the Great Migration. Despite being away from the south's more overt racism, poor and working-class Blacks looking to start a new life are introduced to the more systemic and subtle forms of racism like home and loan denial and exceptionally high interest rates. This is due to now 34 years of Racially Restrictive Covenants **(See #45, #49, #88)**. But they are at least working "good" factory jobs. *Watch what happens 20 years later* **(See #76)**. And in the cases when the covenants aren't applied to Blacks moving into a home or apartment, they are met by a different kind of racial restriction—being bombed out of their homes by the police and angry White mobs, like **Harvey and Johnetta Clark** in Cicero, Chicago. [277]

## 60. 1954.

The young, unknown, freshly graduated preacher Martin Luther King, Jr, moves his new wife, **Coretta Scott King (See #60, #65, #74, #82, #88)** to

Montgomery, Alabama. He's accepted the job to take over as lead pastor of Dexter Avenue Baptist Church. At the same time, Malcolm X, two years removed from prison, is leaving Detroit to accept the position of Chief Minister of Temple No. 7 in Harlem, New York. Over the next five years, he will spearhead the Nation of Islam to more than 40,000 members and 49 temples. Meanwhile, while the NOI is demanding racial separation and civil rights leaders fight for desegregation, 17 states want no parts of integration and keep racial segregation on the books. That is until **Brown v. Board of Education** lands in a Topeka, Kansas courtroom. Thurgood Marshall is back on the case 11 years after winning a major political victory in *Smith v. Allwright* **(See #55)**. And on his legal team is a professor from Howard University School of Law, Spottswood Robinson **(See #55)**. Ten years later, he is still holding on to his old student Pauli Murray's **(See #54, #55, #62)** graduate argument on using the 14th Amendment to overturn segregation. As he and Thurgood prepare their statements, it's decided that Murray's collegiate argument will be used. And it works. She was right all along. [278]

*Throughout most of history, men, Black or White, have always received the spotlight and the credit for women's presence, participation, and innovation – the troubles of Jane Crow.* Fifty-eight years later, the Supreme Court finally overturns *Plessy v. Ferguson* **(See #34)** and finally announces rather supremely that segregation, in public schools at least, does actually violate the 14th Amendment and is therefore unconstitutional. [279][280] *Brown v. Board was a groundbreaking victory. However, White students, teachers, school boards and parents still violently responded to integration. Moreover, it never resolved issues at majority Black schools which were still inferior and under-resourced thanks to a lack of government and state funding and poor redlined communities creating poor redlined school districts. Things will change in 36 years* **(See #84, #93)**.

### 61. 1955. The Murder of Emmett Till.

The Vietnam War begins and over 300,000 Black men fight for... freedom? **(See #9, #19, #28, #31, #39, #44, #54, #58, #84, #87, #100)**. [281][282][283] Black soldiers — "Soul Brothers" — find a new solidarity in the jungles of war and create "the dap" handshake. *The creatively rhythmic and coordinated handshakes is an acronym -* **"Dignity and Pride."** Back in the south, 15-year-old NAACP youth council member **Claudette Colvin** is being arrested in Montgomery, Alabama, for refusing to move to the back of the bus. She is pregnant and tired but defiant about her constitutional rights. *Unfortunately, her story of refusal won't be highlighted because an unwed, pregnant teen can't be the face of a movement.* [284] Six months later, another teenager will make headlines, but for a very different reason. While visiting his cousins from Chicago, 14-year-old **Emmett Till** is brutally murdered and found in Money, Mississippi's Tallahatchie River. After allegedly whistling at 21-year-old Carolyn Bryant **(See #94)**, the boy is found with a bullet in the head, his eye gouged out, barbwire wrapped around his neck, and his body weighted down with a cotton gin.

*I hope you're noticing the pattern of Black male violence, White protectionist supremacy, and the use of White women as an excuse for violence. But if not...* **(See #43, #46, #47, #58, #83)**. Emmett's mother **Mamie Till** decides to have an open-casket funeral. She wants the world to see what they did to her baby boy. The two White men who grabbed him, Roy Bryant and J.W. Milam, boast about the murder and are still acquitted by an all-White jury in 67 minutes **(See #44, #46, #51, #53, #57, #58, #67)**. One juror said, "If we hadn't stopped to drink pop, it wouldn't have taken that long." With Emmett Till's death, the **Civil Rights Movement** officially begins. *Norris v. Alabama* **(See #53)** *does nothing for Emmett Till, and Blacks are still not judged by a jury of their peers. This is still relevant to why every single protest still happens.* [285] [286] [287]

## 62. 1956. "Eliminate the Black Messiah."

Nine months later, the Montgomery, Alabama chapter of the NAACP finalizes its boycotting plans. Because the group believes Claudette's pregnancy **(See #61)** will bring unwanted negative attention, they decide to go with their 43-year-old secretary **Rosa Parks** instead. Following Parks's orchestrated arrest, Jo Ann Robinson and the Women's Political Council send out thousands of leaflets calling for a one-day boycott of the city's buses. [288] The young pastor, Dr. King, also gets a call. He is requested to lead the citywide movement on behalf of the Montgomery NAACP and the Montgomery Improvement Association. They need a fresh face. Someone the police don't know. And in his own way, he needs a chance to believe he can do something about what happened to Maceo Snipes **(See #57)**.

With that, the **Montgomery Bus Boycotts** begin. King enlists the help of CORE **(See #55)** and the King of Calypso, **Harry Belafonte**, to bring national attention to the nonviolent protests. Celebrities have been used to bring attention to protests for decades. After the boycott begins, young Claudette Colvin finally gets her moment. She testifies as one of the five key plaintiffs in **Browder v. Gayle** to challenge bus segregation in Montgomery. Ten months later, the Supreme Court orders Montgomery and the state of Alabama to end bus segregation. After 381 days of boycotting city buses, walking and carpooling, the Montgomery Bus Boycotts ends. Dr. King crowns the historic moment by being one of the first to sit in front of the now-integrated bus. [289][290] The victory against segregation in Montgomery leads to the beginnings of a more strategic plan to desegregate the nation **(See #63)**. *Butterfly Effect Moment: Martin Luther King moves to Montgomery six months before Claudette Colvin is arrested. Still too new and unknown at the time, if the NAACP goes with young Claudette instead of waiting nine more months for Rosa, King maybe never gets his chance to take the lead, and not only does his entire life trajectory change, but also that of the entire Civil Rights Movement. Ann Pauli Murray, still busy trying to tear down the walls of Jane Crow, accepts a job at a prestigious law firm in New York and inspires a young intern named* **Ruth Bader Ginsburg (See #100)**. *Fifteen years from now, Ginsburg will use one of Murray's legal articles to argue that the 14th Amendment's Equal Protection Clause applies to women in the 1971 case Reed v. Reed.*

**Nat King Cole** becomes the first Black American to host a primetime show on national television (NBC). After 64 episodes, the show ends because companies did not want Black people marketing and selling their products. Meanwhile, **FBI Director J. Edgar Hoover (See #42, #43, #62)** monitors the events in Alabama, Harlem, and on his television screen. America is changing, and he's determined not to let that happen. *Sounds like more Great Replacement, right?* And in the same way Hoover targeted alleged Communists and Black nationalists like Marcus Garvey 37 years ago **(See #45),** he is now establishing a top-secret agency within the FBI known as the **Counterintelligence Program - or COINTELPRO** for short **(See #63, #70, #71, #74, #75, #77, #78, #79, #81, #100).** The stated goal of the secret agency is similar to his previous assignment with the Radical Division: (1 Maintain the White U.S. status quo, meaning all White and all male-dominated, (2) Monitor and detain domestic "radicals," and (3) Break up all counterculture protests movements. But he adds two more: (4) Investigate high-profile cases but never convict anyone **(See #58, #68, #69)** and (5) **"Eliminate the Black Messiah" (See #67, #70, #74, #75, #83).** [291] [292] [293] [294]

**63. 1957.**

Driven by the success in Montgomery **(See #62)**, **Martin Luther King Jr, Bayard Rustin, Ella Baker (See #42, #64, #67), Ralph Abernathy, and Fred Shuttlesworth** finalize their plans to combine isolated desegregation movements under one organization. They call it the **Southern Christian Leadership Council (SCLC)**. The goals: Abolish legalized segregation in the South and end the violent disenfranchisement of Black southerners. [295] In Harlem, Malcolm X is speaking out against police brutality after the NYPD brutally beats **Johnson X Hinton**. In the same way Montgomery put Martin in the spotlight, the media coverage in New York brings Malcolm national attention, including by the FBI and COINTELPRO. They label him a **"key figure" for surveillance**. Five months later, nine Black students courageously take part in a major test to see if the recently passed *Brown v. Board of Education* **(See #60)** actually works. They volunteer to desegregate Central High School in Little Rock, Arkansas. After facing riots, angry mobs, and blockades by the Arkansas National Guard, President Dwight D. Eisenhower enacts Executive Order 10730, and the **Little Rock Nine** are escorted to class by the 101st Airborne Division and 10,000 federalized troops. [296] Six days later, and only after Senate Majority Leader Lyndon B. Johnson **(See #69)** passes his watered-down version, President Eisenhower signs the **Civil Rights Act of 1957**. This act allows federal prosecution of anyone who tries to prevent someone from voting *(on paper, not in practice)* and establishes the Civil Rights Division in the Justice Department. [297] [298] *Remember when I said the Enforcement Acts of 1870* **(See #35)** *would come back around 87 years later? Here we are, back around again.*

*But in total, it took 92 years to get here. This is the first act since 1865 to specifically address Black civil rights and signaled the U.S. government's gradual acknowledgment of the growing movement.*

## 64. 1960. The Emmett Till Generation.

Like the Little Rock Nine, more teenagers and young adults are braving discrimination. This time in North Carolina. In February, **the Greensboro 4** sit down in peaceful protest at a local Woolworth's diner. Protest is dangerous, but it works. Months later, they can now order and eat at the newly integrated counter. [299] The former NAACP leader, founder of the NACW **(See #42)**, and now SCLC coordinator **Ella Baker** wisely acknowledges the Greensboro movement and realizes realizes the potential of a nation full of Black teenagers and college students who are affected not only by the death of Emmett Till but the not guilty outcome of the trial. *Sound familiar?* Two months later, Baker taps into that spirit and creates the **Student Nonviolent Coordinating Committee (SNCC).** [300] The new group is meant to let the young folks join the fight and determine their own future and will include a young and fired up **John Lewis (See #70, #99), Diane Nash, James Bevel, Marion Barry, Bob Moses, Julian Bond, Fannie Lou Hamer (See #44, #69), H. Rap Brown, and Stokely Carmichael (See #70, #71, #73).**

**65. Also in 1960.**

**The 90-Second Call that Changed a Presidency and Political History.** October. Six months after SNCC is organized, Martin Luther King, Jr. finds himself sitting in a jail cell for the umpteenth time in Dekalb County, Georgia. He and 51 other members of SNCC were arrested for participating in a sit-in protest at a "Whites-only" restaurant and department store. At the very same time as his arrest, the 1960 presidential race is happening between Democratic Massachusetts Senator **John F. Kennedy (See #68)** and **Richard Nixon (See #77, #78, #79)**, the Republican Vice President for the current president, Dwight D. Eisenhower **(See #63)**. They both need the Black vote, and they both know the one person to call. Both JFK and Nixon are hesitant, too worried it would decrease votes among White voters. Even after Jackie Robinson **(See #54, #57)** tries to convince him to help their friend King, Nixon says he can't risk it. But Kennedy decides he will. He calls Coretta Scott King and Martin Sr. to gain their approval, and 30 hours later, King is released. Two hours later, King tells the media he is indebted to Kennedy for his support. The following month, 70% of Blacks voted Democrat for the first time. Out of 68.3 million votes, JFK wins the presidency by 118,574 votes. **Thanks to the Black vote.** [301] *Butterfly Effect Moment: Before JFK makes that phone call, more than 40% of Blacks were still Lincoln Republicans, which is why Jackie Robinson, a Republican, talks to Nixon. Even King, who did not consider himself a member of either party, was closer to Nixon than Kennedy.*

*But after he failed to help, King called Nixon a "moral coward," and their relationship was over for good. This one moment changed the demographic of the Democratic Party into what we see today.*

**66. 1961.**

After returning to the NAACP **(See #42)** and being subsequently kicked out for believing that socialism, not gradual American integration, was the only option for Black liberation and equality, W.E.B. Du Bois joins the **American Communist Party**. He then moves to Accra, the capital of Ghana, at the request of the country's first prime minister and president, **Kwame Nkrumah (See #73)**. *Of note, many Black Americans joined and sided with Communist groups and ideologies. Quite simply, they treated them as equal and recognized them as human, a stark contrast from the allegedly democratic ideologies America proclaimed itself to own.* Back in the south, the **Tougaloo Nine** is working to desegregate libraries in Jackson, Mississippi. After clashes with the police, jail time, fines, and hundreds of students showing up to support, the libraries are ordered to desegregate. [302] Months later, CORE and SNCC organize the Journey of Reconciliation 2.0 **(See #57)** to fully desegregate busing in Alabama. *Yes, again. Because everything is on paper, not in practice.* This initiative comes to be known as **the Freedom Rides**. After the integrated riders face bombings, arrests, and beatings by angry White mobs, the Interstate Commerce Commission prohibits transportation segregation everywhere. [303]

One victory after another, nonviolent protests is working its desegregating expelliarmus magic. *That's a Harry Potter reference. High five if you got that. Oh, and on paper, not in practice. That's an American reference. High five if you've realized, thus far, that nothing is changing.* And up north, Malcolm has just been named the National Representative of the Nation of Islam - second in command behind leader Elijah Muhammad. This move stirs resentment among several in Muhammad's circle who do not want him to be the next leader **(See #68, #69, #70)**.

**67. 1962-1963.**

While Dr. King's SCLC and Ella Baker's SNCC plan more nonviolent strategies, police units across the country are making counter-demonstration plans. **Police militarization increases**, especially in Los Angeles, as the city moves towards its two largest riots **(See #70, #85)** and anywhere racial protests occur. As a result, **riot and SWAT teams are created**. [304] While King is trying to figure out nonviolent solutions against "Whites-only" policies and police brutality, the south continues to prove why it's so hard to bring change. Reminiscent of Maceo Snipes **(See #57)**, KKK member Byron De La Beckwith murders WWII veteran, civil rights activist, and NAACP field secretary **Medgar Evers** outside of his Jackson, Mississippi home. The FBI or the local police were known to follow Evers every day except the day of his murder. Beckwith is later arrested and acquitted by an all-White jury **(See #44, #46, #51, #53, #57, #58, #61). "Not Guilty."**

But *we'll have to wait another 32 years for a resolution* **(See #86).**

## 68. 1963. King's Dream and a Bombing in Birmingham.

W.E.B. Du Bois passes away in Ghana just one day before the march begins. *Du Bois was one of the most prolific modern Black intellectuals of his time and ours. He authored 17 books, founded four different journals, and clearly defined how the experiences of America and Black America could be understood and why they mattered for societal progress, justice, and equality. More than that, he believed in the "Talented Tenth," the idea that one in ten Black men had the potential and the ability to become leaders of the Black community for the Black community by acquiring a college education, writing books, and becoming involved in social change directly. His legacy and this ideology, "For Us, By Us," continues to thrive today among Black men and women.* One day later, Martin Luther King shares his **"Dream"** with 200,000 people at the Lincoln Memorial while the D.C. police, Hoover's FBI, some 2,000 national guardsmen, and 19,000 Army soldiers are on standby -This is known as **"Operation Steep Hill."** [305] *Martin Luther King's "I Have A Dream" speech will go on to be ranked number one in the Top 100 Speeches of the 20th century.* [306] One month later, four members of the United Klans of America—Thomas Blanton, Herman Cash, Bobby Cherry, and Robert Chambliss—bomb the **16th Street Baptist Church** in Birmingham, Alabama, sending sending shock waves through the country and completely reversing any feelings of progress and momentum from the March on Washington. After the smoke has cleared, four young Black girls have been found dead in the rubble. The bomb detonated near the church basement and right next to where the girls were getting dressed for Sunday school. **Addie Mae Collins (14), Cynthia Wesley (14), Carole Robertson (14), and Denise McNair (11)**. So angered, Dr. King sends a telegram to the extremely racist and segregationist Alabama governor, George Wallace: **"The blood of four little children is on your hands."** The FBI investigates. The names of each man involved are sent to Hoover, but no convictions are ever made. In fact, Hoover blocked any prosecutions against the suspects and refused to discuss the case. Two months later, President John F. Kennedy, the same man who took the risk to free King from jail to secure the Black vote and began drafting the Civil Rights Act, is **assassinated in Dallas**, Texas. With disagreements boiling and relationships souring, Malcolm X makes disparaging remarks about Kennedy's assassination, calling it **"a case of chickens coming home to roost."** *Translation: America had killed so many Black people and let them get away with it, and now this was their karma.* This remark gets him demoted and silenced by the NOI. Soon after, he makes another shocking public announcement that changes his fate forever: Elijah Muhammad has engaged in repeated adultery and has children with at least three NOI secretaries. **This is the final straw**. Members loyal to Elijah Muhammad begin making plans to oust Malcolm X for good while the FBI and COINTELPRO listen, plan, and orchestrate in the background.

## 69. 1964. "I Question America."

With guidance and advice from Malcolm, heavyweight champ Cassius Clay joins the NOI and changes his name to **Muhammad Ali**, but their friendship ends soon after. Why? Because after 11 years of dedicated service and increasing membership by the thousands, the Nation of Islam suspends Malcolm X indefinitely. And Malcolm can sense the danger. **"They're going to kill me soon."** Following a debate at the University of Oxford in England, he meets with a journalist friend, Tariq Ali, and privately tells him either **the FBI or the NOI (or both)** will murder him, and they won't be meeting again. [307] Despite the worry of death, he establishes his own Islamic-based, pan-African and universal movement called **the Organization of Afro-American Unity (OAAU)** and holds weekly meetings at the Audubon Ballroom **(See #70)**. Malcolm also gives one of his most famous speeches while visiting Cory Methodist Church in Cleveland, Ohio, *The Ballot or the Bullet*. In the speech, he advises Blacks to exercise their right to vote, but he also cautions that if the government continues to prevent Black Americans from attaining full equality, it may be necessary to take up arms. [308] *This speech will go on to be ranked number seven in the Top 100 speeches of the 20th century.* [309] Back in Washington D.C., leader of the Mississippi Freedom Democratic Party Fannie Lou Hamer **(See #44, #64)** tells the Democratic National Convention, **"I Question America."** [310] [311]

Hamer's speech directly challenges White supremacy, voter suppression and racist violence and attempts to persuade Congress to pass a law protecting the rights of Blacks to vote in the south. *Her speech will go on to be recognized as one of the bravest speeches ever given by an activist.* As if she never spoke, the Mississippi police and the KKK murder **James Chaney, Michael Schwerner, and Andrew Goodman** two months later. The men were kidnapped, beaten, shot and buried for conducting voter drives on behalf of the **Freedom Summer** campaign to increase Black voter registration in Philadelphia, Neshoba County, Mississippi *"Mississippi Burning"*. The FBI investigates. No one is indicted or convicted. [312][313][314] This is also the same month **Monson Motor Lodge** manager James "Jimmy" Brock pours acid into his hotel pool to force out a group of Black and White protesters in St. Augustine, Florida. Dr. King was arrested at this same hotel a week before for trying to desegregate its restaurant. [315] Three weeks later, on July 2, President Lyndon B. Johnson begrudgingly pushes the Civil Rights Act of 1964 to a vote. After passing in the House, Malcolm X travels to D.C. to observe the Senate vote on the act. **Either by happenstance or divine providence, Malcolm X and Martin Luther King Jr. run into each other**. Although they disagree on many subjects— Malcolm once referred to Martin as "a 20th century or modern Uncle Tom" **(See #24)** for his nonviolent, civil disobedient approach—there is mutual respect between the men. A photographer takes their photo while they embrace and share a laugh. **It will be the only time these men will ever meet.** [316] [317]

Soon after, the **Civil Rights Act of 1964** passes in the Senate, and 89 years later, this act finally reverses the 8-1 Supreme Court decision in the Civil Rights Act of 1875 and prohibits discrimination of ALL kinds and in ALL places **(See #36)**. *On paper, not in practice. Y'all have seen me state that quite a few times now. And we're not done yet. But it only took Emmett Till being murdered, Montgomery buses being boycotted, SCLC and SNCC sitting in and boycotting, Greensboro Fours, Tougaloo and Little Rock Nines, Medgar Evers being murdered, 200,000 marching on Washington, four little girls being murdered before Sunday school, Fannie Lou calling out America's hypocrisy on national television, Freedom Riders and Freedom Summers, a hotel owner throwing hydrochloric acid in a pool and two White men and a Black man being murdered in Mississippi while getting people to vote and COUNTLESS other acts, arrests, beatings, and murders for a president's signature. Why must we do so much, die so much, and sacrifice even more for the most basic requests in life?* And for his strivings, including the tiresome work of the individuals around him, Martin Luther King Jr. accepts the Nobel Peace Prize by the end of the year. He will be the second Black person to receive the award after Ralph Bunche **(See #58)**.

**70. 1965. An Assassination in the Audubon.**

A year prior, Malcolm X made the Hajj to the Kaaba in the Holy City of Mecca, Saudi Arabia. He prayed next to "pilgrims of all colors" and returned a changed man. Most particularly, he changed his views regarding

White Americans and advocated for their place in this fight for Black equality. But while he is safe and celebrated abroad, at home in New York was a very different story. Like Medgar Evers **(See #67)**, Malcolm has a personal detail of FBI and NYPD that follow him daily, but not today. February 21. Today is too quiet. Just before going on stage to give a speech, Malcolm tells one of his personal ministers that he "really shouldn't be here today." His house had been bombed seven days before. Men were at his hotel lobby asking for his room number the day before. Today, on the drive to **Manhattan's Audubon Ballroom** for his OAAU meeting, the usual cops were nowhere to be seen. But the people needed to hear the message. As soon as Malcolm takes the stage, a man yells,**"GIT YO HAND OUTTA MY POCKET!"** - a signal for the assassins to attack. A man throws a smoke bomb in the crowd to cause panic while four men walk down the aisle towards Malcolm shooting him with shotguns and pistols. The 39-year-old Malcolm X is assassinated in front of his pregnant wife, children, and followers **(See #63, #68, #69)** Talmadge Hayer **(See #92)**, Norman 3X Butler, and Thomas 15X Johnson **(See #100)** are arrested. Hayer confesses to his role in the crime and tells the courtroom that Butler and Johnson were not involved, but he refuses to name his co-conspirators or who hired him. [318] The jury is not convinced. The Nation of Islam is blamed publicly. The COINTELPRO is heavily involved secretly. And the remaining details are shrouded in mystery. [319 320 321]

Seven months later, Black author Alex Haley **(See #80)** publishes **The Autobiography of Malcolm X**, which goes on to be a bestseller. While the nation mourns, the Black Codes **(See #31)** still suppress the Black vote in the south, forcing SCLC and SNCC to do their best to increase voter registration. In Lowndes County, Alabama, **Stokely Carmichael (See #64)** is angry with Dr. King and the SCLC leadership and their nonviolent strategies, especially after Malcolm is killed. While field organizing Black voter registrations, he establishes his own political party, **the Lowndes County Freedom Organization (See #71)**. And because all political organizations need a logo, Carmichael chooses the **Black Panther**, which will inspire two young men all the way in Oakland, California **(See #71)**. But in Selma, Alabama, things are about to turn bad — **Bloody Sunday** bad. Everything changes for the worst when **Jimmie Lee Jackson** is killed by Alabama police while trying to protect his mother during a protest. Following the incident, **John Lewis (See #64, #99)** and **Hosea Williams** prepare to lead 600 protesters on a 54-mile walk from Selma to the capital of Montgomery to desegregate the city and demand voter rights for Alabama's Black residents. As the group crosses the Edmund Pettis Bridge, named for a Klan Grand Dragon, they are stopped by the Alabama police, told to turn around, go back across the bridge, or face the worst. The protesters remain still and begin to pray, which is soon interrupted by violent beatings. The brutality is televised nationally, stirring many White viewers to answer Dr. King's call for volunteers.

*This is one reason why Dr. King was so adamant about nonviolence.* *He understood that White people needed to see themselves act in this type of violent behavior against peaceful and law-abiding citizens to bring about change.* Two days later, **Pastor James Reeb, Viola Liuzzo**, and many other White citizens are moved by the images and travel to Selma to help. The very first night he is there, a mob of White men severely beat Reeb and two other ministers. [322] The Black hospitals did not have the services to treat him and the White hospitals refused to take him in. Because of the delay, Reeb went into a coma and died two days later. Two weeks later, Liuzzo is shot and killed by Klan members (and one FBI undercover informant) while driving Black voter registrants. [323] [324] **Liuzzo's death signaled the first time the federal government investigates the KKK since the passing of Ulysses S. Grant's Ku Klux Klan Act of 1871 (See #35).** Feeling pressure from the violence in Selma, President Johnson introduces the **Voting Rights Act of 1965**. Dr. King joins Lewis and Williams to march those 54 miles from Selma to Montgomery the second time around. After completing their journey, President LBJ signs **the Civil Rights Act of 1965** so Blacks can finally vote with federal protection. *On paper, not in practice. but for the first time since the first Angolans were brought to Winyah Bay, South Carolina, in 1526* **(See #1)**, *and since the Slave and Negro acts defined them as "property"* **(See #5, #6, #8)**, *and since the Supreme Court said they would never be human or citizen in the 1857 Dred Scott case* **(See #6, #25, #33, #37)**, *and since all kinds of Klan violence, lynchings, poll taxes, literacy tests,* *property tests, and grandfather clauses, finally the American African is both human and citizen with federal voter protection (kinda). That was 57 years ago.* Additionally, poll taxes **(See #46)** are declared unconstitutional thanks to ***Harper v. Virginia State Board of Elections***. But the celebrations are cut short just five days after President Johnson signs the act, because LAPD officers have just pulled over 21-year-old Marquette Frye for suspected drunk driving in Los Angeles. While detained, he is struck in the face with a baton **(See #67)**. The abuse against Frye, mixed in with a rumor that the police kicked a pregnant onlooker, set the Watts community on fire for six days. The state deploys nearly 14,000 California national guardsmen to help suppress the disturbance. In the end, there were 34 deaths, 1,000 injuries, 4,000 arrests, and $40 million in property damage. [325] The **Watts Riot** would be LA's worst until … **(See #85)**.

## 71. 1966.

While the *Brown v. Board of Education* behind-the-scenes architect Pauli Murray **(See #54, #55, #60, #62)** is establishing the **National Organization of Women (NOW)**, [326] Dr. King is in his eleventh year of activism and even more frustrated with the slow change of America. President Johnson is beyond angered with him for speaking out against the Vietnam War and not answering or returning any of his calls. Dr. King also faces another growing ideological issue among Black activists:

too many are being killed or beaten, and the days of the nonviolent movements are quickly becoming unpopular. The old ways of doing things just aren't appealing, especially to the young folks. He's constantly at odds with SNCC and arguing with his own people. He wants to quit. With all he's done and all the progress he's made, the Black-nationalist-by-any-means-necessary-don't-you-dare-turn-the-other-cheek ghosts of **Martin Delany (See #24), Marcus Garvey (See #44), and Malcolm X (See #69)** comes back from the beyond and looms over King's nonviolent attempts. **"We Want Black Power!"** In June, Stokely Carmichael **(See #64)** begins the militant, self-defending Black Power Movement after **James Meredith** is shot during **"The March Against Fear"** - the 220-mile march from Memphis, Tennessee to Jackson, Mississippi, to raise awareness for Black Mississippi voter oppression. [327] One month later, comic writers **Stan Lee and Jack Kirby** introduce the first Black superhero, **T'Challa, a.k.a. The Black Panther**. They're inspired by the Civil Rights Movement, Marcus Garvey, and **Mansa Musa**, the Mali Emperor and the richest man ever to live. In October, in Oakland, California, college students **Huey Newton and Bobby Seale** are tired of the brutality and violence of the police in California and at the same time find inspiration from Stokely's Black Power and Lowndes County Black Panther movement. So inspired, they establish the **Black Panther Party for Self Defense**, an alternative to the nonviolent protest of the south and one that combines Black Power with political knowledge, anti-colonialism, anti-capitalism, and armed self-defense to protect Blacks against police brutality and violence. [328] [329] [330] [331] The following year, the Panthers raise their national recognition when they escort Malcolm X's widow, **Mrs. Betty Shabazz**, during her visit to San Francisco. Yes, T'Challa predates this group. In actuality, he was briefly known as The Black Leopold to create distance, but the new name didn't stick, thankfully. Three months later, and in direct response to this new political group in Oakland, the open carry state of California passes the **Mulford Act, a.k.a. "The Panther Bill."** This bill outlaws the public carrying of firearms. **Governor Ronald Reagan (See #81)** signs this bill into law after 26 Panthers show up at the capitol building armed in protests. *See what happens when way too many Black folks walk around legally carrying. Gun laws change very quickly.* The Black Panthers are now on Hoover's FBI/COINTELPRO radar and begins its investigations into the organization **(See #73, #75, #78, #83).**

**72. Also in 1966.**

The Supreme Court introduces **"Qualified Immunity"** to protect officers from "frivolous lawsuits" **(See #89)**. [332] [333] *Relevant for the next 56 years.* In the same way Abraham Lincoln needed more soldiers during the Civil War **(See #28)**, the U.S. is once again in need of more men to fight in the now 11 year war in Vietnam **(See #61)**. As a result, the government enacts **"Project 100,000,"** and judges ask Black men, **"Jail or Vietnam?"**

During the war, Black soldiers were assigned to the most dangerous units, accounted for 25% of all deaths, and were the most incarcerated in U.S. military prisons in Vietnam like Long Binh Jail. [334][335] Also, congressional reports state that heroin addiction is growing among Vietnam veterans **(See #78)**. [336][337] Angered by the Vietnam War and the lack of economic progress for poor Blacks and Whites, Martin Luther King Jr. begins organizing his last movement, **the Poor People's Campaign (See #74)**. [338]

**73. 1967. "When the Lootin Starts, The Shootin Starts."**

After 178 years of the Supreme Court's existence and years of court battles and civil rights victories, **Thurgood Marshall becomes the first Black appointee to the Supreme Court**. In Miami, Police Chief Walter Headley is testifying at a hearing regarding crime rates in the city and tells the committee, **"When the lootin' starts, the shootin' starts."** That same year, during another speech, Headley said his "Get Tough" policies were, in fact, a "war on young hoodlums, from 15 to 21, who have taken advantage of the civil rights campaign… [and we] don't mind being accused of police brutality." His legacy and statements will come back around in 53 years **(See #97)**. Similar rhetoric is echoed in Detroit during the **"Detroit Rebellion,"** the largest riot in America at that time since New York residents robbed, killed, and looted during the Draft Riots in 1863. After the Detroit police department raid the Black-owned Blind Pig bar, a race riot ensues for five days resulting in 43 dead, hundreds injured, 7,000 arrested, and 2,509 buildings destroyed by fire or looting. [339] After stepping down as SNCC president to become an Honorary Prime Minister of the party he helped inspire, Stokely Carmichael **(See #64, #70, #71)** is kicked out of the Black Panther Party after the COINTELPRO conducts a disinformation campaign and sends a letter to the Panthers that Stokely is a CIA agent. [340] With very serious threats to his life, he moves to Guinea, Africa, with the blessings of Kwame Nkrumah **(See #66)**, and changes his name to Kwame Ture **(See #87)**. [341]

**74. 1968. A King is Killed.**

No longer satisfied with just voting rights, Dr. King plans his Poor People's Campaign, and he believes the ongoing labor movement in Memphis, Tennessee, exposes the need for economic equality. The sanitation union workers call him to organize the strike, and he agrees to help. After a bomb threat holds up his plane in Atlanta, a feverish and unusually nervous King checks into the Lorraine Motel with his entourage in Memphis. His room is supposed to be on the first floor, but Memphis police request he move to the second floor, to Room 306, to protect him better. Allegedly. Eight hours later, **James Earl Ray** checks into the New Rebel Hotel under the alias "Eric S. Galt." Later that night, while giving a sermon at Mason Temple Church, King tells the packed room,

"I've been to the mountaintop. I've seen the promised land. I may not go with you. But I want you to know tonight that we, as a people, will get to the promised land." The next day, Ray hears King is staying at the Lorraine over the radio. He checks out of his room and checks into a nearby hotel, this time as "John Willard." His room has a perfect line of sight to Room 306. Dr. King is standing on the balcony and joking around with **Jesse Jackson and Andrew Young (See #78)**. James Earl Ray aims his rifle out of the bathroom window. A single loud shot rings across the parking lot. King is rushed to the hospital, unconscious but still alive, though barely. Some say doctors did everything. Others say doctors did nothing and let him die. *Either way, this is also one of many reasons Blacks do not trust hospitals or science* **(See #50, #51, #57, #59, #79, #97)**. One hour after being shot, Dr. Martin Luther King Jr. is pronounced dead. Like Malcolm X, King was also 39 years old. His autopsy revealed he had the heart of a 60-year-old due to the stress and fighting for civil and economic rights for 13 years. Two days later, Mrs. Coretta Scott King gives a speech saying her husband's "spirit will never die"(See #82). [342] **The King Assassination Riots** occur in over 200 cities across America for 53 days straight. Amidst the riots, police kill 17-year-old Black Panther **Lil' Bobby Hutton**, literally two days after King is killed. And as one last ode to Dr. King, President Johnson signs the **Fair Housing Act of 1968** seven days later. [343]

The act prohibited discrimination concerning the sale, rental, and financing of housing based on race, religion, national origin, sex, handicap, and family status. *Yeah, you got it – on paper, not in practice* **(See #91, #93)**. *It only took 157 years (since 1865), but Blacks can finally vote, buy a house, and be legal American citizens trying to make a living with federal protection. On paper, sometimes in practice. Again, I need you to realize that was only 54 years prior to the publication of this book.* Two months later, James Earl Ray is caught in London. He is named the lone shooter, but Mrs. King immediately suspects the FBI **(See #43, #47, #48, #50, #52, #54)**. *Given their history and all the "anonymous" letters they sent to her, why wouldn't she?*Four months after Ray's capture, Tommie Smith and John Carlos are suspended from the U.S. Olympic team for raising Black-gloved fists at the summer games in Mexico. Their act attempts to bring awareness to Black poverty and those who have been lynched or killed. [344]

## 75. 1969. Black History Month.

January 3. After successful protests for increased Black History classes and Black faculty, Black Union Students at **Kent State University** demand to extend Dr. Carter G. Woodson's Negro History Week to celebrate the first **Black History Month (See #49, #79)**. [345] Imitating their success, colleges across the nation begin hosting their own Black History Month celebrations. Eight months later, **Angela Davis**, a Black Panther, political activist, and educator, is added to the FBI's Most Wanted List.

The third woman ever to be added. [346] [347] Around the same time, **Richie Havens** opens Woodstock with "Freedom," and **Jimi Hendrix** shuts the music festival down. Two Black musicians begin and end the inaugural year of **Woodstock** in New York in front of 400,000 attendees. One day later, Angela Davis's comrade Bobby Seale is arrested in Berkeley, California, for allegedly inciting a riot at the Chicago Democratic National Convention, beginning the **Chicago Eight trial**. Later, it was changed to the Chicago Seven after Seales's case was declared a mistrial. That same year, 1969, J. Edgar Hoover pledges that the end is near for the Black Panther Party. He devotes most of the FBI's resources to ensure it happens. Using secret agents, sabotage, misinformation, and lethal force, the FBI creates internal rivalries by sending fake letters and causing trust issues, all of which ruin Huey P. Newton mentally**(See #78, #81)**. With Hoover waging his secret "by any means necessary" war with the Panthers, the war soon takes its heaviest toll. While the Chicago Eight are on trial in Downtown Chicago, Deputy of the Black Panther Illinois chapter **Fred Hampton** is drugged to sleep by CIA informant William O' Neal and assassinated by Chicago police and the FBI on the north side of Chicago. *Watch Judas and the Black Messiah for a Hollywood reference.* Police conduct the raid at 4:30 am, firing 82-99 shots through doors, walls, and windows. Despite the ballistics report detailing only one shot was fired from the Panthers, the police still claim self-defense, and no one is ever indicted or convicted. *By now, the pattern should be quite obvious – Not Guilty.*

## 76. The 1970s.

The now deceased Victor Hugo's Green Book ceased publication three years earlier, but **Gladys Mae West,** a real Hidden Figures mathematician, has just built the model which will become the basis for the Global Positioning System. *Yes, that GPS.* [348] In the meantime, The Great Migration is finally slowing down after 60 years of Black movement **(See #38, #42, #61)**. More than six million Black Americans have left the south. Far from the lynching and Jim Crow laws, they find another struggle now as technology, globalization, and outsourcing increase Black unemployment to 20% **(See #59). Low education, no job opportunities, and a poor, redlined public housing environment leave the door wide open for crime, drugs, and increased police activity at the behest of the state and federal governments**. Congress also passes the Comprehensive Drug Abuse Prevention and Control Act, allowing officers to conduct **"no-knock" searches**. Thanks to the FHA, homeownership for White families has skyrocketed by more than 60%, while low-income project neighborhoods continue to be the norm for Black families across the country. Although the times look more than grim, more Black politicians are elected, offering a glimmer of hope for Black America. One of those Black representatives, **Shirley Chisholm (See #77),** becomes the first Black woman to join Congress and the first woman to run for the Democratic presidential nomination. Although she hopes to make change, there's a war coming ...

*****

# WARMONGER

# CHAPTER IV:
# 1971-2007

# The War on ~~Drugs~~... Blacks

*The Warmongers. The Get-Tough-on-Crimers. The Law and Orderers. The vanguard of the drug war. The disregarders of Black circumstance and systemic tragedy.*

*Crime rates are historically high, and a political crisis is brewing. Gangs and gun violence, drug use among children, "welfare queens," and the crack cocaine epidemic floods newspaper and television headlines. There's unrestrained fear in every suburban corner of America, and the public is in a frenzy, believing they will be the next victim. They demand something – anything – to be done. Yet, without any real solutions, lawmakers arrive at only one conclusion:*

*Mass incarceration.*

*The more arrests and prosecutions, the longer the prison sentences, the fewer the criminals, the drugs, the violent activity.*

*And then the safer the country. Or so their thinking goes. The goal is worth the cost. And the cost falls heavily on the Black community. Single-parent households increase because fathers have been arrested, killed, or have left their responsibilities at the door. The young are left to raise themselves, and whispers from the streets grow louder. Some make it out. By luck, maybe. The rest are left to survive in the haunted shadows with the damned and dangerous in the part of town America never takes you to on its tour. Denial is an easier pill to swallow. And instead of rehabilitation and addressing the root causes, they choose the torturous nightmare of war.*

*The Slave Codes, Negro Act, and Black Codes. The active hindrance of Black advancement. The racially restrictive covenants and denied suburban homes. The public housing projects. The high rates of unemployment. The redlined communities and schools that keep property values low until they're ripe for gentrification. Crack cocaine. The increase of police militarization and the subsequent harsh punishments only to fill the privately-owned prisons, justify the raised mandatory sentences and judicial kickbacks, and ultimately limit all opportunities for felons upon their exit, so recidivism rates continue the cyclic nature of... War.*

**This is the Warmonger Era.**

## 77. 1971. COINTELPRO Ends. War on Drugs Begins.

Using the Muhammad Ali vs. Joe Frazier fight as cover, an anti-FBI group known as the Citizens' Commission to Investigate the FBI raid a small FBI office in Media, Pennsylvania. The group ransacks the entire building and steals more than 1,000 highly classified documents. Hoover sends more than 200 agents on the hunt to find these robbers, but it's too late and of little consequence. The group has already leaked the information to the media. **For the first time since 1956, J. Edgar Hoover's destructive COINTELPRO is publicly exposed and terminated (See #43, #47, #48, #49, #50, #54).** [349] [350] [351] As a result of the Supreme Court's racism, state-sanctioned segregation efforts, and the political suppression you've read about in the last 76 posts, **the Congressional Black Caucus (CBC)** is established by 13 Black leaders that include Shirley Chisholm, Bill Clay, Ralph Metcalfe **(See #53)**, John Conyers, and Charles Diggs, the only member of Congress to attend the "trial" for the murder of Emmett Till **(See #61)**. Their mission is to politically advocate on behalf of Black Americans **(See #99)**. [352] [353] The CBC offered President Richard Nixon 61 strategic recommendations and how-tos on eradicating racism, providing quality housing for Black families, and promoting the full engagement of Black citizens in government. [354] Instead of implementing these recommendations, Nixon, who initially refused to meet with the CBC, just like he refused to call Martin Luther King, Jr. **(See #65)**, does the reverse and sparks the **"War on Drugs."** [355] The war will go on for the next 48 years and will also be presided over by the next nine presidents. [356]

## 78. 1972.

Although the "War on Drugs" initially sought to increase prevention and treatments for drug abuse (methadone clinics, education campaigns, etc.), it eventually shifts resources to law enforcement and criminalization. Nixon implemented the Republican Party's **"Southern Strategy"** to increase White conservative voter support in the south and realign political demographics by appealing to racism against Black Americans, women's places in society, and White Christianity. [357] He also created the Office for Drug Abuse Law Enforcement *(a precursor to the Drug Enforcement Agency)* specifically to focus on Black crime. [358] Again, Black men are targeted, and arrest rates soar. Reminiscent of the Convict Leasing System **(See #32)**, mass incarceration begins again, and police militarization presence in inner cities increases even more **(See #67)**. One example of the increased militarization is occurring in West Philadelphia *(Don't sing it. I know you couldn't help yourself, but don't.)* against the Black liberation group known as **MOVE (See #81)**.[359] Elsewhere, Huey Newton is extremely paranoid. His co-founder, Bobby Seale, has his eye on a mayoral seat in Oakland and is on the verge of leaving the Panthers. Believing everyone works with the CIA or FBI and heightened by the Stokely Carmichael incident, Newton just doesn't know who to trust anymore and thinks everyone is out to get him. As a result of effective COINTELPRO strategies over the past six years, Huey begins shutting down chapters nationwide **(See #75)**. And more than 70 years later, **Barbara Jordan (Texas) and Andrew Young (Georgia) (See #74) become the first Black Congressional representatives from the south since 1898.** *Yes, the same year, Black politicians were forced out of town during the Wilmington Massacre* **(See #39). Young is also the first Black Congressman for Georgia since 1865.** *Yes, the same year slavery ended as an institution.*

**79. 1973-1976.**

The **Drug Enforcement Agency (DEA)** is created. Following New York Governor Nelson Rockefeller's lead, Nixon proposes harsher prison sentences, including mandatory minimum sentences for drug traffickers and users. While Nixon is dealing with the Watergate scandal and beginning to ramp up Black convictions, J. Edgar Hoover dies just two years after the exposure and termination of COINTELPRO **(See #77)**. *He left a legacy of establishing the federal guidelines on how to dismantle Black movements; breaking up Black families; targeting independent and diverse thinkers as well as political activists; assassinating Black leaders, all while indirectly supporting local police and Klan violence through sham investigations and non-convictions that significantly undermined the overall gains and momentum of the fight for civil rights, justice, and equality in America.*

New FBI Director Clarence Kelley apologizes to the American public for the abuses inflicted during Hoover's 54-year reign. [360] But for the Black community en masse, the damage has been far too much, and the trust in police institutions is forever lost. Dr. Martin Cooper invents the mobile cell phone two years later, but its usefulness won't be revealed for another 25 years **(See #87)**. After 45 years, North Carolina finally ends its sterilization program **(See #50). Around 7,600 women are sterilized in total. Of those sterilized, 40%were minorities. Of the 40%, most were Black women or young Black girls**, like 13-year-old **Elaine Reddick**, who was raped by her neighbor, taken to the hospital, blamed for being "promiscuous" and "feeble-minded," then sterilized after a c-section. *Another reason Blacks do not trust hospitals or science* **(See #50, #51, #57, #59, #74, #97)**.[361 362 363] The eugenics program was eliminated in 1974, but legislation permitting involuntary sterilization remained on the books until 2003. [364] With Watergate forcing Nixon out of office, the new president, Gerald Ford, is pressured by a national collegiate effort spearheaded by the Black students at Kent State University to federally designate the month of February as Black History Month. *Just like the movements of SNCC* **(See #64)**, *college kids make yet another significant change for America. So no, "they" didn't "give us the shortest month of the year." Dr. Carter G. Woodson organized the week in February* **(See #49)**, *the Kent State students celebrated for a month* **(See #75)**, *and college students created a Black history movement that nationally focused on expanding Black history curriculum and hiring Black faculty, pushed it to the forefront to get the president's signature. Own it.*

## 80. 1977-1978. The Roots of Affirmative Action

The miniseries *Roots: The Saga of an American Family* airs on national television for eight consecutive nights. Alex Haley's **(See #70)** mini-series spans more than 115 years and is the first to show viewers the impact of the transatlantic slave trade and the institution of slavery on American society. The show also receives 37 Emmy Award nominations, nine wins, a Golden Globe, a Peabody, and was the second-most watched series in U.S. television history. In California, *UC Regents v. Bakke* secures a historic victory. The Supreme Court rules that a school's use of racial "quotas" in its admissions process was unconstitutional, but **affirmative action** to accept more minority applicants is acceptable and can be used to address past discrimination. *Because of the 79 other things listed before this.* [365] Thanks to the Voting Rights Act of 1965 **(See #70)**, there is a significant increase in Black elected officials. In the south, the number of Black officeholders, like Barbara Jordan and Andrew Young, grow from 100 in 1964 to 4,300 in 1978 **(See #78)**.

## 81. 1980-1981. A Bombing in Philadelphia.

Black Harvard law professor **Derrick Bell** leaves the university after leading protests to bring Black issues to the intellectual forefront. One of Bell's Black female [366] graduate students, **Kimberlé Williams Crenshaw**, continued his legal debates and demonstrations, which become the origins of **Critical Race Theory (See #99)**.

After defeating Jimmy Carter in the 1980 presidential election, movie acting-former California governing-Black Panther muzzling-Mulford Act signing **Ronald Reagan** is now president **(See #71)**. *He receives 14% of the Black vote.* He, too, continues the "War on Drugs" and even outdoes Nixon. With the growth of the private prison industry, [367] **the Corrections Corporation of America** is founded, and prisoners become a Wall Street stock (CXW). [368] Elsewhere across the world, the Black Panther Party for Self Defense officially ends, largely due to the invasive, incarcerating, and murderous tactics of COINTELPRO **(See #48, #50)**. *After 16 years of challenging police brutality and violence, the Panthers also successfully established 48 chapters across the U.S. and chapters in Europe, Asia, and Africa. They organized 35 community survival and free breakfast programs and provided education centers, libraries, and after-school programs for kids. They offered tuberculosis testing, legal aid, transportation assistance, ambulance services, and distributed resources to poor. They fought for the self-determination and survival of Black communities and have been forever immortalized.* In Texas, the state declares Juneteenth a state holiday, 115 years after Granger arrives in Galveston **(See #22, #30, #100)**. And in Philadelphia, the police arrest several MOVE members and then orders the rest of the group out of their compound **(See #78)**. The group decides not to leave until the police release their members. However, even after release, the group stays put, arguing their legal right to be there. The police arrive in full riot gear, inciting a shootout between the two groups. After their patience wears thin, a police helicopter drops two one-pound bombs on the MOVE compound, destroying 65 row houses. Numerous arrests are made, and 11 MOVE members are killed. Five are children. The mayor offers an apology, but no one is ever convicted. [369]

**82. 1983-1985. Snowfall.**

Mrs. Coretta Scott King and Stevie Wonder are at the White House watching President Reagan sign **Martin Luther King Jr. Day** into federal law. *"His spirit will never die"* **(See #74)**. *Ironically, Dr. King would have protested exhaustingly against this president signing his name into the holiday records.* This same year, **Alice Walker** wins the Pulitzer Prize for fiction for her book, *The Color Purple. Two years later, Steven Spielberg directs the film adaptation starring Oprah Winfrey, Danny Glover, and Whoopi Goldberg, who wins the Golden Globe award for Best Actress.* The following year, Nancy Reagan's "Just Say No" movement begins. While publicized as a message for everyone, it primarily focuses on White, middle- class children. At the same time, the **Iran-Contra Affair** is taking place. Ronald Reagan and officials within the National Security Agency, the FBI, CIA, and U.S. State Department are backing Nicaraguan rebels fighting communism. They're also secretly supplying weapons to Iran to fight Iraq while turning a blind eye to the drugs imported into the U.S. [370 371 372 373 374] *Whoo! That is a scandalous mouthful!* As a result, crack cocaine destroys inner cities and their residents. *The FX show "Snowfall," created by the late and great John Singleton, is a fictional show based on actual non-fictional events.*

**83. 1986-1989. The Ghost of Willie Horton.**

As crack cocaine continues to rise in Black and Brown neighborhoods, Reagan signs **the Anti-Drug Abuse Act of 1986**. The bill allocates $97 million to build new prisons and, at the same time, enhances mandatory minimum penalties for drug offenses. Possession of at least one kilogram of heroin or five kilograms of cocaine is punishable by at least ten years in prison. [375] This is the beginning of the Black versus White, crack versus powder cocaine, sentencing disparity **(See #82, #84, #86, #91, #96)**. [376] Drug arrests increase 126% when the 1988 presidential elections kick off. Republican and former vice president to Ronald Reagan, **George H.W. Bush**, runs a campaign based on "Get Tough" policies. He also runs the racially charged **Willie Horton ad**. *Willie Horton was a prisoner who raped a White woman from Maryland and tied up and stabbed her boyfriend while released on a furlough program.* Bush uses Horton's story to show Democrats were weak on crime **(See #85)**. He channels Thomas D. Rice **(See #21, #84, #97)** to stereotype Black men, instilling more fear and duplicating the White protectionist supremacy tactics by insisting on the vulnerability of White women **(See #43, #58, #61)**. [377] [378] [379] Reminiscent of the Scottsboro Boys **(See #51)** and Groveland Four **(See #58)**, the case of the **Central Park Five** also adds to the Willie Horton fears as five Black boys sit in prison for the alleged attempted rape and murder of a White woman jogging through Central Park, New York. In response, real estate mogul **Donald Trump (See #94)** buys an entire op-ed space in the New York Times newspaper to write, "Bring back the death penalty. Bring back our police!" Bush will go on to win the presidency against Massachusetts Governor Michael Dukakis with 11% of the Black vote. After multiple stints in jail and dealing with FBI-induced paranoia and all chapters of the Black Panther Party shut down, 47-year- old **Huey P. Newton (See #75)** is murdered by a West Oakland gang member during a drug deal. *Long after exposure, this is only one example of the unfortunate and damaging effects of the FBI's COINTELPRO.*

**84. 1990. 100-to-1.**

After years of failed pitches, inventor and Air Force veteran **Lonnie Johnson's Super Soaker** finally breaks toy records, netting $200 million in sales and ranking in the top 20 best-selling toys. Elsewhere in America, the National Race and Politics Survey publishes its findings on race relations in America: **59% of Whites believe Blacks lack discipline; 31% believe they are lazy; 56% believe Black women prefer to live on welfare, and 50% believe they are prone to violence.** [380] These beliefs are all due to decades of society upholding negative stereotypes introduced by the likes of Thomas D. Rice, Thomas Dixon, and D.W. Griffith **(See #43, #44)**, as well as scientific racism **(See #21)**,

Willie Horton-type generalizations, increased police militarization, and mass incarceration justifying their "lack of discipline, laziness, and violence." With stats like these, George H. "Dub-ya" Bush continues the same "War on Drugs" and proposes to add an additional $1.5 billion to the cause. **Congress also passes a 100-to-1 sentencing disparity for crack rock (Black) and powder cocaine (White) (See #83, #100).** This results in vast racial disparities in sentencing because most Whites used the more expensive cocaine powder while inner-city Blacks used crack rock. Black prisoners faced longer sentences for crack cocaine than offenses involving the same amount of powder cocaine—two forms of the same drug. [381] Additionally, Blacks served just as much time in prison for nonviolent drug offenses as Whites did for violent offenses. *This sentencing pattern will go on for another 24 years and affect millions of prisoners* **(See #91).** Bush also adds a 50% increase to military spending. Why? Because across the water in a small country called Kuwait, the Gulf War (Desert Shield/Desert Storm) begins. And it comes to a swift end one year later. But more than 100,000 Blacks fight for… freedom? **(See #9, #19, #28, #31, #39, #44, #54, #58, #61, #87, #100).** [382] Back stateside, court rulings release the desegregation orders, effectively bringing an end to the legacy of *Brown v. Board of Education* **(See #60, #63, #90, #93).**

## 85. 1991-1992.

California On Fire. March 3, 12:45 a.m. **Rodney King** is leading the LAPD on a high speed chase through Los Angeles. Eight minutes later, he pulls over and is charged with driving under the influence of alcohol. Once in police custody, four police officers—three White, one Hispanic—brutally assault King, kicking him and beating with their batons for 15 minutes while more than a dozen other officers stand by and watch. King suffers skull fractures, broken bones and teeth, and permanent brain damage. A bystander records 89 seconds of the beating on a personal video camera, later broadcast on the news in every home across the nation. [383] Ten days later, on March 13, Korean store owner Soon Ja Du fatally shoots 15-year-old **Latasha Harlins** in the back of the head. Latasha entered the convenience store to buy a $1.79 bottle of orange juice, which Du thought she was stealing. After she lay dead, Du realized Latasha had $2 in her hand. While Black America awaits the trials in LA, Thurgood Marshall **(See #55, #57, #60, #73, #99),** the first Black man to sit on the Supreme Court, officially hangs up the robe in June due to his declining health. President Bush taps **Clarence Thomas (See #100)** to fill the role as the second Black man to sit on the Supreme Court. But he must first get through a grilling testimony regarding the sexual assault of **Anita Hill** and media pressure about his right-winged activist wife, **Virginia "Ginni" Thomas (See #98).** [384] In November and back in California, Soon Ja Du is defending herself in court and claims "self-defense." Using surveillance footage from the store, the jury finds her guilty of voluntary manslaughter. But instead of serving a maximum of 16 years, the judge empathizes and sentences her to five years of probation, 400 hours of community service, and a $500 fine. [385] *LA's powder keg is almost lit...* Five months later, in April 1992, Rodney King's trial begins. This time the jury is somewhat mixed: nine Whites, one biracial male, one Latino, and one Asian. And even with video evidence, it still does not matter. All four cops are acquitted. Less than three hours later, the **"Not Guilty"** verdict sparks LA's largest riot since the Watts Rebellion **(See #70)**. *And the largest American riot of the 20th century.* The death toll reaches 50, including ten who were shot and killed by the LAPD and California National Guard. Some 2,000 are injured, most notably the truck driver Reginald Denny. Nearly 6,000 people are arrested, and 3,000 buildings are destroyed or damaged, totaling one billion in property damage. Of the damaged buildings, 65% were Korean-run businesses and included Soon Ja Du's store. [386][387] *Still relevant to protests and riots. To most, what might be one isolated incident is a very long, tiresome, and angering history of Black America. Hopefully, you see that now.* Seven months later, the polls are in, and the "First Black President" defeats George H.W. Bush. **Bill Clinton** becomes president, winning 83% of the Black vote. *Minus the fact that he was from Arkansas, played the saxophone and was perceived as a clear contrast from Bush, I have no idea why Black folks christened Bill Clinton with that nickname. But that's also an example of what happens ~*

*when you don't really see what's going on around you at the moment, and then history paints a very different story for you later.* To show he's not a Democrat that's allegedly weak on crime **(See #83)**, he, too, like Bush, Reagan, Carter, Ford, and Nixon, continues the "War on Drugs," police militarization, and the mass incarceration of three million Blacks. *But when the economy is up and doing well, who really pays attention to all that, right?* As a show of strength, Clinton enacts **the 1033 Program**, which transfers just over five billion dollars worth of excess military weapons to law enforcement, giving police forces tactical weapons, grenade launchers, and mine-resistant ambush-protected (MRAP) vehicles - the same trucks used in Afghanistan and Iraq to protect U.S. Soldiers from explosive terrorist weapons. [388][389] *If this doesn't signal an actual war in America, I don't know what does.*

**86. 1994-1995.**

KKK member and assassin Byron De La Beckwith is retried 31 years later after new evidence is found. And 31 years later, he is finally convicted of the murder of Medgar Evers **(See #67)**. *Let me remind you he killed this man in broad daylight in his driveway for trying to get Black people in Mississippi to vote.* In March, California introduces **Proposition 36, the Three Strikes Act**, to "keep murderers, rapists, and child molesters behind bars, where they belong." But more than half of those trapped by the law are nonviolent criminals. Over 45% of inmates serving life sentences under the Three Strikes law are Black **(See #92)**. [390] **The Violent Crime Control and Law Enforcement Act,** the **1994 Crime Bill**, is also introduced by **Senator Joe Biden (See #99, #100)**. [391][392] The law imposes harsher and longer prison sentences at the federal level and encourages states to do the same. Because state prisons hold more than 86% of the prison population, the bill sets aside exclusive federal funding for states that: (1) Choose to build more prisons, (2) Fund 100,000 more cops, (3) Support programs that encourage police officers to carry out more drug- related arrests, and (4) Adopt truth-in-sentencing laws which effectively increase prison sentences by requiring prisoners to serve at least 85% of their time before the possibility of parole. [393][394][395] *I know that all sounds terrible, and it was, but it was primarily for federal prisoners because, contrary to popular belief, the 1994 Crime Bill didn't affect STATE prisons and jails. As a federal law, it focused on federal prisoners, so the mass incarceration of Black males is really a direct result of state policies, loosely influenced by federal guidelines and monetary incentives. There is much blame to go around, including the arrested individuals. However, the blame also falls squarely on state convict leasing ideological policies, enforced mandatory minimums, and racially charged police militarization of low-income communities and has lingering effects today.* While prison sentences are getting tough, **John Ehrlichman**, Watergate co-conspirator and former campaign and domestic policy advisor for former President Richard Nixon **(See #78)**, meets with journalist Dan Baum for an interview to explain how the "War on Drugs" (and Blacks) began. He states the following:

"The Nixon campaign in 1968, and the Nixon White House after that, had two enemies: the antiwar left and Black people. You understand what I'm saying? We knew we couldn't make it illegal to be either against the war or Blacks, but by getting the public to associate the hippies with marijuana and Blacks with heroin, and then criminalizing both heavily, we could disrupt those communities." [396] One year after this interview, the U.S. Sentencing Commission (See #90, #95) notices the racial disparities between Whites and Blacks and crack and powder cocaine and recommends reducing the discrepancy (See #83, #84). For the first time, Congress overrides their recommendation. The "War on Drugs" keeps chugging along. [397] The reduction in sentencing, which the commission recommends, won't happen for another 13 years (See #91).

**87. 1998-2001.**

Kwame Ture, formerly known as Stokely Carmichael and the man who started the Black Power movement and inspired the Black Panther Party, dies of prostate cancer in Guinea. [398] James Earl Ray also dies in prison from liver and kidney disease. Coretta Scott King addresses her deep sadness for Ray's death and the tragedy that they will never know what actually happened on April 4, 1968 (See #74). The 2000 Census finds that segregation between Blacks and non-Blacks declines dramatically for the third straight year. [399] This news sounds good on the surface. However, gerrymandering increases to maintain political domination. Speaking of politics, **George W. Bush** keeps the family business going and wins the election after a questionable Florida recount debacle. He defeats Al Gore, former vice president to Bill Clinton, and wins 9% of the Black vote. In 2001, Oklahoma finally recognizes the **Tulsa Race Riot and the Burning of Black Wall Street** 80 years later **(See #46)**. *But no one has ever been prosecuted, nor have reparations been rewarded. Acknowledgment without justice is irrelevant.* **September 11, 2001. Osama Bin Laden** and his new terrorist organization known as **Al Qaeda** orchestrate a multi-city attack in the United States. President G.W. Bush promises revenge, and the Global War on Terror begins. [400] More than 500,000 Blacks are serving in the military and still fighting for... freedom? **(See #9, #19, #28, #31, #39, #44, #54, #58, #61, #84, #100)**. [401] And thanks to Dr. Cooper's cell phone invention **(See #79)**, Samsung and Sharp introduce the first camera phone. This invention will place the destruction of Black bodies on full viral display and help ignite a movement in a few years **(See #92)**. As if these were the years the FBI decided to catch up on old racist cases like De La Beckwith, they officially reopen and close the file on the 16th Street Baptist Church bombing in Birmingham, Alabama. The FBI arrests two of the four White men involved — Thomas Blanton and Bobby Cherry. Thirty-eight years later, both men are found guilty and given four consecutive life sentences **(See #68)**. [402] *Robert Chambliss was convicted in 1974 and*

*died in prison eight years later, and Herman Cash died in
1994 without having ever been tried.*

## 88. 2005-2007. This Was Planned.

New Orleans, August 23-31, 2005. **Hurricane Katrina** is
one of the worst natural disasters in American history.
After the city's levees collapse and the flood-protection
system is compromised, 80% of New Orleans is now
underwater. More than 110,000 homes and another
20,000 businesses are destroyed, and 1,800 people are
dead. Black and poor communities are hit the hardest.
Black homeowners in New Orleans are more than three
times as likely to have been flooded as White
homeowners. That was not due to bad luck. This was
planned. It is the result of decades of racially
discriminatory policies and housing practices,
redlining, and racially restrictive covenants **(See #45,
#49, #59)**. [403] [404] *This underscores the ignorance of the
Supreme Court when they opined in the Plessy v. Ferguson
decision that physically separating people did not make
things inferior* **(See #38)**. *How racist. How wrong.* During
New Orleans' early developmental years, the higher
ground and areas less susceptible to environmental
damage and flooding were reserved for White families.
Once the banks began loaning higher interest loans to
those who wanted to buy a home, Black families found
themselves in less desirable, less economically valued
parts of the city. It was only a matter of time. After
Katrina hits, the city rebuilds White areas first and
faster. Black areas remain in disrepair or

THE BLACK LIST: 1526 - 2022

have been completely lost. [405] [406] Almost 100,000 Blacks leave New Orleans and never return to the city. During a fundraising campaign for Katrina victims, **Kanye West** says on live tv, "George Bush doesn't care about Black people." *Translation: George Bush was simply a metaphor for New Orleans and Louisiana state policies and American anti-Black policies in general. Basically, he surmises that "America doesn't care about Black people."* And up north in Kanye's hometown of Chicago, Illinois, the city council finally cares at least about one Black person. After 227 years, the council officially names **Jean-Baptiste Point du Sable the founder of Chicago (See #16)**. They also draw up plans to erect a statue on Michigan Avenue near the same spot as his old front door. This same year, Mrs. Coretta Scott King passes away from ovarian cancer in Rosarito, Mexico. She was more than a wife. And after taking the lead role for her husband following his assassination in Memphis, pushing for a federal holiday, and expanding the movement to include women and the LGBT community, she is respectfully crowned **the First Lady of the Civil Rights Movement**.

*****

# ILLUSIONS

# CHAPTER V:
# 2008-2022

# Illusions of a Black President and The Myth of a "Post Racial" Society

*Illusions and delusions of grandeur. Instead of taking historical lessons from John Willis Menard's Louisiana, Hiram Revel's Mississippi, or Joseph Rainey's South Carolina. Instead of checking on Shirley Chisholm's New York, Barbara Jordan's Texas, or Andrew Young's Georgia. We celebrated the promotional first. A well-deserved applause indeed, as they made their demands known for the cause of the Black plight within a system so rooted in anti-Blackness and so counterproductive to collective Black advancement.*

*What changed? What remained? Or was it just the simplistic appeal of seeing someone like you sitting somewhere like there? Who let you in? You're not supposed to be there. But indeed, you are. What a sight! What a moment! But the pitfalls of race-baited politics are many. And while the audience distracts themselves with celebratory mirages, the crowd unconsciously or intentionally dismisses the harsh realization of seeing who we still are after the last of the confetti is swept up at the end of the night.*

*See, Jackie Robinson never ended racism in baseball; he merely exposed it, much like the actual first Black president of the United States. And given the history of Black history, the moniker alone is magnanimous. The responsibility? Even more. The thinnest of rope, the shortest of leash, and the impossible balancing act of attempting to please the unpleasable and those waiting for your every mistake. There is no room for mistakes. The illusion we tell ourselves is that maybe, tokenism matters more than we think. Because things will be different this time. It must be different. Things are changing, right? We pray. They prey.*

*We want the illusion of a post-racial society to match the reality of still being very much a racialized, politicized, historically mischaracterized, and male-centralized society. And we create this myth for ourselves to coddle our realities, while history writes itself like a madman only to reveal our authentic appearance when we are ready to commit to opening that chapter. Like Jackie, a Black president never changed America. It simply showed us more of who we had always been. A nation of celebrated first and little substantive change…*

**This is the Era of Illusion and Myth.**

## 89. 2008. An Actual First Black President.

In arguably the most historic presidential race ever, **Barack Obama** defeats John McCain with 95% of the Black vote and moves his belongings into the house built and re-built by the enslaved **(See #14, #17, #19)**. But while Black people celebrated a bit too much and too long, they missed what was actually going on during his first term. Like Bill Clinton and the rest of his predecessors, he continued the "War on Drugs" and the increased militarization of the police through the 1033 program **(See #85)**. [407 408] Qualified Immunity **(See #72)** is also on the rise in cases involving excessive or deadly force by police. And then, just like in 1929 **(See #50)**, Wall Street crashes again, thanks to a housing bubble. [409] The Dow Jones drops by 777 points, the largest drop in history. The Great Recession also begins, and the average American loses their job and savings and is financially destroyed as they find themselves owing more on their mortgage than the house is worth. [410] *See Adam McKay's film "The Big Short" if you need a Hollywood reference.* While Americans receive $600-$1,200 stimulus checks, Wall Street, insurance companies, and the Big Three automakers (General Motors, Ford, and Chrysler) are bailed out with billions. [411 412] *Surprisingly, no one ever calls this "reverse welfare" or a handout.* Not so surprising. Black people and Black business owners are hit the hardest, [413] leading to a horrifying statistic: **Black median wealth and income are projected to be zero by 2053.** [414 415] *Again. A very, very long history of restrictive* *covenants, FHA exclusionary policies, high interest rates, lack of homeownership, and owning less valuable homes in less desirable areas until gentrification forces them out and they are offered less for what will soon become exponentially more.*

## 90. 2009.

In the same city where Huey Newton and Bobby Seale hoped to bring about change against police brutality and violence 43 years before, **Oscar Grant** is killed by police in Oakland to start the new year. After pleading the shot was an accident and that he meant to grab his taser, officer Johannes Mehserle receives a sentence of less than one year. *Watch Michael B. Jordan portray Oscar Grant in "Fruitvale Station" and try not to cry.* Elsewhere in D.C., President Obama nominates **Ketanji Brown Jackson (See #91, #100)** as the Vice Chair of the U.S. Sentencing Commission **(See #86, #95)**. It's a historic promotion for a Black woman, but it won't be her last.
[416] This happens at the same time hate crimes fall in the U.S., but Blacks are still more likely than any other racial or ethnic group to be the victims of those crimes. While unemployment levels dropped for all groups, Blacks are still nearly twice as likely to be unemployed as Whites.
[417] [418] [419] Blacks are still less likely to have health insurance. Thanks to the end of *Brown v. Board of Education* **(See #84)**, public schools are segregated again, and Black and minority schools are still underfunded. Foreclosures, housing discrimination, and predatory lending against Blacks, Asians, and Hispanics continue

during a global recession. Drug use and drug dealing is rampant throughout Black communities, specifically, maintaining a very active police presence. [420] *Illusions and myths of a post-racial society...*

## 91. 2010.

Obama signs the **Fair Sentencing** Act thanks to the work of the U.S. Sentencing Commission and its new Vice Chair KBJ **(See #90, #100)**. [421] Finally, 24 years and more than three million prisoners later, the crack-cocaine disparity tied to the "War on Drugs" is reduced **(See #83, #84, #86)**. But is it too late? Prisons are still overwhelmed. More are being built, and police still heavily patrol the inner city. *Yes, obviously, where there is crime, there is police, but the key is to understand how the inner city got this way.* This is also the year the **"Kids for Cash"** scandal is exposed. Judges had received financial kickbacks for imposing harsh sentences and increasing private prison rates. [422] Wells Fargo is also exposed for restricting "ghetto loans" to Black "mud people." It's also reported that Blacks have the highest loan denials of all races— 25% —while Whites are denied at 10%. [423] This adds to why Black households nearing retirement (age 55-64) had just a fourth of the savings held by White families. Numerically speaking, Blacks held an average of $30,000 while Whites owned $120,000. [424] And while Blacks are being denied homes, Talmadge Hayer, one of the many involved in the 1965 assassination of Malcolm X, is now released on parole after serving 44 years **(See #70)**.

## 92. 2012. The Trayvon Martin Generation.

In the same way Emmett Till's death and the "Not Guilty" verdict for Roy Bryant and J.W. Milam stirred the nation into the 1950s and 60s Civil Rights Movement, the death of Trayvon Martin and the "Not Guilty" verdict for George Zimmerman ignited the **Black Lives Matter Movement.** *Point of clarification: Black Lives Matter can mean two very different things. It can either refer to the organization or the cultural movement, which is completely detached from the organization, but simply believes in the words and meaning of "Black Lives Matter." Please do not conflate the two.* The movement will find itself protesting a very long list of names over the next few years: **Eric Garner. John Crawford. Ezell Ford. Michael Brown. Tanisha Anderson. Laquan McDonald. Tamir Rice. Sandra Bland. Renisha McBride. Freddie Gray. Alton Sterling. Philando Castile. Samuel Dubose. Meagan Hockaday. Aiyana Jones. Rekia Boyd. Jeremy McDole. Walter Scott. Terence Crutcher. Korryn Gaines.** [425] And ultimately hearing a lot of **"Not Guilty"** verdicts. The same cell phone Dr. Martin Cooper created and Samsung / Sharp camera fixtured is now capturing murders in vivid display and sharing those images worldwide. But, like Rodney King's video 20 years before, this is still not enough to convict officers of wrongdoing. In some cases, officers receive pay raises like Daniel Pantaleo, who killed **Eric Garner** with an illegal choking hold. Garners' last words were, **"I Can't Breathe."** In response to the Black Lives Matter protests, "All Lives Matter" and

"Blue Lives Matter" is coined to show "support" for police officers. [426] *This is referred to as a red herring distraction tactic. A red herring is something that misleads or distracts from a relevant or important question. By the way, if "All" lives matter, Black lives also must matter, by the definitional default of "Black" being included within the word "all." Anywhoo...* To amend the previous 14 years, California passes the Three Strikes Reform Act **(See #86)**. The act eliminated life sentences for non- serious, violent crimes and established a procedure for inmates sentenced to life in prison for minor third strike crimes to petition for a reduced sentence. As a result of the act, more than 1,000 inmates are released in the first eight months.

## 93. 2013-2015.

President Obama's second term. This one is much different, highlighted by his comfort in singing Al Green's "Let's Stay Together." He accomplishes 55% of his promises to Black Americans this time around. Black unemployment declines slightly. Black median income increases by 4.1%. He is the first of 43 presidents to visit a federal prison. And he launches the "My Brother's Keeper" and "Advancing Equity for Women and Girls of Color" initiatives to address the opportunity gaps Black boys and girls face. [427] And while high school graduation rates for Black students reach the highest point in history, with 72.5% graduating, those same "Blue Lives" and their congressional backers continue the war. In 2013, FBI reports reveal White drug use at 9.5% and Black drug use at 10.5%, but only 332 Whites per 100,000 residents were arrested compared to 879 Blacks. Also, per judicial tradition, Blacks still face longer prison sentences than their White counterparts when arrested. [428][429] A 2015 Sentencing Project report concludes: "A myriad of criminal justice policies that appear to be race-neutral collide with broader socioeconomic patterns to create a disparate racial impact. Policing policies and sentencing laws are two key sources of racial inequality." [430] *Translation: Judicial policies seem race equivalent on the surface, but the "broader socioeconomic patterns," discriminatory policies, practices, and covenants set in place in the past 92 bullets and enforced police activity in Black communities make those same judicial policies very racially biased.* Speaking of discrimination, it's still rampant in the housing and economic sector. Black household average net worth is $138,000 to $933,000 for White families. On average, a White family's net wealth is seven times greater than a Black family. *Brown v. Board of Education* really, really ends **(See #60, #63, #84)**. [431][432] Schools are resegregated, and "Apartheid Schools," schools that are 99% Black, increase, especially throughout inner cities and lower economic communities. [433] And in Charleston, South Carolina, White supremacist Dylan Roof is walking into the Emanuel African Methodist Episcopal Church.

## 94. 2016. "Make America Great Again..." But For Who?

The Republican Southern Strategy is revived **(See #78)**. The economy has bounced back since the Wall Street Crash of 2008. The era of the nation's first Black president is coming to an end, and race relations are generally bad right now, with 70% of Black America saying it has faced racial discrimination; 47% has experienced someone suspicious of them; 40% say their race has made it harder to succeed in life and police have unfairly stopped 21%. [434] **And after eight years of Barack Obama at the helm, 43% are doubtful the U.S. will ever achieve racial equality.** [435] *Illusions and myths.* At the same time, Hillary Clinton loses the presidential race, stirring arguments for changes to the Electoral College **(See #13, #17)**. Donald Trump ushers in the "What do you have to lose?" and "I've done more for the African American community than any president, with the exception of Abraham Lincoln" era. "Make America Great Again" essentially embodies the same effect *Birth of a Nation* **(See #43)** had on certain White populations in 1915. With the not-so- coincidental rise of racial division, White extremists and  White supremacists' rhetoric in the country increases, [436] [437] [438] [439] starting with hate crimes going up by 200% in cities where Trump held rallies. [440] [441] Meanwhile, in Santa Clara, California, **San Francisco 49ers safety Eric Reid and quarterback Colin Kaepernick** sit down on the bench in protest during the "National Anthem" **(See #51)**. After speaking with **Army Green Beret Nate**

**Boyer** and learning from him what kneeling represents at military funerals, **Kaepernick takes a knee** for the first time at the next game. Not in disrespect to the military or veterans. Not even in disrespect to all police. Just against the terrible, violent, "he reached for my weapon self-defense," and "Not Guilty," but actually very guilty ones **(See #92)**. And during the "national" song, that was written during slavery (1814) by an enslaver, Francis Scott Key, and poetically takes a jab at enslaved people being killed as they tried to escape for freedom during a war (of 1812) **(See #19, #51)**. *And because silently protesting 490 years of social injustice in America and police and mob violence actors being acquitted when brutality, violence, and murder happens is a right we should all understand.* Speaking of unjust violence and murder, the now 82-year-old **Carolyn Bryant** admits to an author that she fabricated the entire story about Emmett Till **(See #61)**. [442] Had she said this 61 years ago, Emmett Till would have been 75 years old, and Carolyn Bryant maybe wouldn't be the only one still alive today.

**95. Also in 2016.**

The Center for Disease Control reveals its data on pregnancy-related deaths: out of 100,000 live births, 42 Black women die, which is more than three times the rate of White women. Disparities in access and quality of healthcare pre- and post-pregnancy play a factor. [443] The U.S. Department of Education and EdBuild reveal their data on schools: the majority of non-White schooldistricts spent $2,000 less per student on average than districts spent $2,000 less per student on average than the mostly White school districts because local property taxes finance schools. Nationwide, that equates to $23 billion. They also reveal the 16% gap between Black and White students who have bachelor's degrees has remained steady for almost three decades (1990-2020), setting up many for a lifetime of social and economic disadvantages and, sometimes, a life of crime. [444] *You can thank segregated, redlined, gerrymandered, underfunded schools for that.* The FBI reveals its data on homicide: 90% of Black homicides were committed by Black people while White people committed 84% of White homicides. *Translation: This is called* **Intra-Racial violence.** *You kill who you live around. Translation to the Translation:* **"Black on Black Crime" is another red herring distraction** when discussing options for police interaction and violence when dealing with Black communities. FBI data also reveals Blacks are three times more likely to be killed by police than White people, even though they are 1.3 times more likely to be unarmed. *Most of this is attributed to negative stereotypes of Black people, Black men in particular, and a long antagonistic history of Blacks versus the police, often originating within mutually disrespectful encounters.* The U.S. Sentencing Commission adds to this by reporting that Black males receive 20% longer prison sentences than White males for the same crime. [445] Remember Onesimus from Boston? **(See #7)** Yeah, I know it was more than two centuries ago, but the African who taught the White preacher about inoculation and how to heal smallpox? Yes, him. Well, he finally gets his recognition and credit! After 220 years, Boston Magazine votes him "#52 Best Bostonian of All Time" (BBOAT) and places Cotton Mather, his owner, five rows down at #57. *Boom! More acknowledgment without justice, but at least he made the list.* Another BBOAT is Malcolm X at #5. *Even though most of his time in Massachusetts was in prison, but I digress.* W.E.B. Du Bois at #9. The 54th Colored Massachusetts Regiment at #15. Phillis Wheatley at #83. Alexander Graham Bell made #17, which really means Lewis Latimer also made #17.

At least Latimer is from Massachusetts. Bell was born in Scotland and raised in London, and he moved to Boston to invent the phone when he was almost 30 years old. [446] *Anywhoo... back to the last few bullets of sadness, madness, and historic gladness. It's been quite a historical journey. Thanks for still being here.*

**96. 2017-2019.**

While a Black woman named **Fawn Weaver** is paying the ultimate homage to Nathan Nearest Green **(See #24, #25, #29)** and debuting the **Uncle Nearest Premium Whiskey brand,** [447] the state of Florida is apologizing to the families of the Groveland Four **(See #58)** and posthumously pardoning the men. The pardon came after the grandson of the Groveland prosecutor found letters proving that his granddad and the sitting judge knew the men had not raped Norma

Padgett. *Acknowledgment, no justice.* Meanwhile, the "Unite the Right" march takes place in Charlottesville, Virginia. A crowd of tiki torch-carrying night light, extreme far right, neo-Confederate "states rights" and Nazi-Germany flag types *(Didn't your grandfather fight against that one?)* crowd rallies to promote the unification of White nationalist movements and protests the removal of the Robert E. Lee statue **(See #30)**. [448] Reminiscent of Viola Liuzzo **(See #70)**, **Heather Heyer**, a Black Lives Matter supporter, leaves the comfort of her home and privilege to fight for Black and civil rights. She is determined to be on the right side of history until she is killed by James Fields Jr., a self-proclaimed White supremacist. Following the tragedy, President Trump channels his inner Confederate Woodrow Wilson echoing, "there were very fine people on both sides" **(See #44)**. [449] While that group avoids jail time (except Fields), the Pew Research Center publishes a report detailing what we already knew: Black Americans still face a higher chance of imprisonment and make up 33% of the U.S. prison population, even though they only make up 12% of the population. By comparison, White people made up 30% of the prison population and 64% of the American people. *White people made up 52% more of the American population, yet Blacks still beat them by three percent of the prison population.* [450] *These are the lingering effects of a 46-year War on Drugs and Blacks.* As a result, more than 7% of the Black population's voting age is disenfranchised compared to 1.8% of the non-Black population. *But they are still counted in the census, which adds to congressional seat representation!* Because of the ongoing and intentional

Black incarceration policies in existence since 1971, **New Jersey Senator Corey Booker, CNN correspondent Van Jones, and Kim Kardashian** (*I bet you didn't think you would see that pop up in here because I didn't either*) persuade President Trump and Senate Majority Leader Mitch McConnell to pass **The First Step Act**. [451] [452] The new law aims to ease the sentences for some crack cocaine-related convictions, shorten mandatory minimums, create a system for inmates to earn credits toward early release, and set up new programs designed to improve their ability to adapt to life after prison. [453] It also ends the practice of shackling pregnant women inmates, gives judges more discretion in sentencing decisions and bans juveniles from being held in solitary confinement. *Watch the Netflix mini-series When They See Us, especially Episode 4.* More than 2,000 people, 91% of whom are Black, receive sentencing reductions because the new law retroactively applies Obama's Fair Sentencing Act of 2010 **(See #91)**. But contrasting this incarceration progress is the reality that Trump appointed the most Appeals Court judges since Jimmy Carter in 1977, and none of them were Black. This has damning effects, not only in the prison sense but also in the political sense, especially in Texas **(See #97)**. Outside the prison walls, the United States Department of Agriculture (USDA) reports that out of every 100 Black households, 21 sometimes have difficulty providing enough food compared to eight White homes. One in ten Black households includes a member who ate less food than they needed because there was not enough money. [454] The CDC also repeats another fact we already knew because it continues to be an ongoing issue: Black adults are more than 1.5 times less likely to have health insurance. *Effects of a history of not being considered human, the result of many Blacks not trusting hospitals or science, and the affordability and lack of access to healthcare services.* In some relieving news, this is also the first year in pageant history that **Miss Teen USA, Miss America, and Miss USA are all Black women — Kaliegh Garris, Nia Franklin, and Cheslie Kryst** *(Rest in Heaven).* But America, and its problems, will soon come to a screeching halt with the arrival of **COVID-19** ushering in a historically angry year.

## 97. 2020. The Ahmaud Arbery, Breonna Taylor, and George Floyd Generation

**The Civil Rights Summer of 2020.** *Full transparency, this was a very emotional and stressful year.* The deaths of Arbery, Taylor, and Floyd inspire protests in all 50 states and across the world. Four years after he was denigrated and slandered for it, everyone, and I mean literally, EVERYONE, is taking a Kaepernick knee. Everyone also includes Nancy Pelosi and the Dems in Kente cloth *(cringe)*, and even police chiefs and police officers in the middle of a Black Lives Matter protest. Every-one. It's weird. But for the first time in a long time, Black culture, Black history, Black demands, and the racist past of the Civil War are pushed to the American forefront. Hard-hat crews take down Confederate statues and lower Confederate flags from flag poles, while any location or building named after Confederacy gets renamed **(See #38, #44, #97, #98)**. The protests also inspire congressional action and push some Senators to try and pass a law that's 98 years delayed. The **Emmett Till Anti-Lynching Bill (See #61)** now replaces the Dyer Anti-Lynching Bill **(See #46, #99)** to make lynching a federal crime with penalties of life in prison. But like the Dyer bill, it too stalls out without resolution after Kentucky Senator Rand Paul refuses to vote, wanting further clarification on the definition of lynching. [455] Meanwhile, across the way in the White House, President Trump says, "Black Lives Matter is a symbol of hate," [456] and gives a "law and order" speech bolstering the actions of police nationwide. He also Ouija boards the racist spirit of Miami Police Chief Walter Headley and tweets, "When the looting starts, the shooting starts" **(See #73)**. [457] Black unemployment is at an all-time low, but so is Black business ownership. Twelve years later and it's still difficult for Black businesses to recover from the 2008 crash. The Small Business Administration (SBA) doesn't help their attempts at resurgence, denying more than 70% of Black-owned small businesses that apply for the Pay Protection Program (PPP). *The PPP allotted $659 billion for small businesses to provide funds to pay up to eight weeks of payroll costs, including benefits and interests on mortgages, rent, and utilities.* The SBA approved 60% of White applicants versus 29% of Black business applications. Those who did get approved for the PPP faced higher interest rates than similar White-owned businesses. [458] [459] [460] [461]

This structural racism led to the closure of at least 40% of Black-owned businesses compared to only 17% of White businesses. [462] And while Black businesses close their doors, the prison gates open theirs as the industry rises 700% since 1980. *Of note, the U.S. has less than 5% of the global population but owns 25% of the world's prison population, of which Black and Brown communities are most affected.* Redlining policies from 88 years ago still affect three out of four Black neighborhoods. [463] Studies reveal Covid-19 disproportionately affects Black people due to redlined living conditions and minimal access to health care. [464] [465] The virus also kills Black people twice as much as Whites. [466] **HeLa cells**, the same ones used without Henrietta Lacks' consent in 1951 **(See #59)**, are still used in vaccine research for Covid variants. *One more reason Blacks do not trust hospitals or science* **(See #50, #43 #51, #57, #59, #74, #79)**. Also, at this time, the wealth gap widens between Blacks and Whites. For every one dollar of accumulated wealth by a White family, a Black family accumulates .01 cents. *Yes, a penny.* [467] And while everything is going on, major companies are trying to correct their own Thomas D. Rice ways by either genuinely or superficially trying to save face with Black consumers. In June, Quaker Oats announces the "Aunt Jemima" brand would be discontinued and replaced with a new image to "make progress towards racial equality." [468] *The same company named after the people who defied the government and set up the Underground Railroad* **(See #11, #14, #24)** *was the same company peddling the* *mammy stereotype for money generations later. The irony!* Following the decision to terminate Aunt Jemima, Nancy Green's **(See #40, #47)** history and legacy is remembered and recognized, but without justice or repayment. Three months later, **Uncle Ben, who was based on Chicago waiter Frank Brown**, is also retired by Mars Incorporated. [469] While the world focuses on Black Lives and changing brand images, Texas Governor Greg Abbott enacts a law allowing only one mail-in ballot drop-off box in each county, severely limiting minority voter accessibility thanks to Trump's all-White, all Conservative appellate judges **(See #96)**. [470] *So much for Smith v. Allwright* **(See #55)** *and the Voting Rights Acts* **(See #70)**.

## 98. 2021. The Biden-Harris Era.

The "If you don't vote for me, you ain't Black" and "You've always had my back, now I'll have yours" Era. Despite answering for the 1994 Crime Bill **(See #86)** and some very questionable, quasi-racist senate speeches, Joe Biden secures 92% of the Black vote and flips key electoral states, including Georgia, for the first time since 1992, thanks to former Georgia gubernatorial candidate, Stacey Abrams. [471] *Once again, Black America saves democracy and America from itself.* And despite having to answer for her mistrustful and contradictory track record with Black male incarceration rates as San Francisco's District Attorney and California's Attorney General, many Black Americans also approve of **Kamala Harris**, ushering in the first Black and Indian and female vice president ever. *This is another landmark moment for American political progress, even though so many other countries worldwide, including those that America believes are "undemocratic" and "uncivilized,"* *have already had female presidents and prime ministers.* But the election is inaugurated with the highest historical drama, with Trump not wanting to leave or lose or face reality. So, misinformation and false allegations of voter fraud and miscounts run rampant. Trump is talking to his closest advisors — Rudy Giuliani, Michael Flynn, and William Barr — about the legality and possibility of using the Department of Justice or the military to take control of ballot boxes in crucial states. [472] Congressional insubordination and hypocrisy become the new norm. MAGA supporters are confusingly cheering "count the vote" in some states and protesting "stop the count" in others. [473] [474] And on the ground in D.C., thousands, including Ginni Thomas **(See #85)**, the wife of Supreme Court Judge Clarence Thomas, [475] are making their way to the nation's capitol to invoke the historic White Supremacist spirit of the Wilmington Massacre **(See #39)** in attempts to overturn the vote through a riot. [476] [477] As the madness unfolds, a noose is erected directly across the street from the Capitol amidst the riot. [478] Five months later, America is still trying to reflect on what happened while the Army begins a three-year review to rename all the bases that commemorate the Confederate States of America and their generals: Fort Bragg, Fort Rucker, Fort Benning, Fort Gordon, Fort Hood, Fort Polk, Fort A.P. Hill, Fort Lee, and Fort Pickett **(See #38, #44, #54, #97)**. [479]

**99. 2022. American Uncertainty.**

January-June 19. COVID-19 has transformed into multiple variants and still managing to discriminate against Black and Brown communities thanks to densely populated neighborhoods with a lack of health resources, a lack of finances, and a healthy mistrust of hospitals. This adds to the troubling list of global supply shortages and historic inflation, rising food, home, car, and gas prices, increased crime across the nation, mass shootings, racist shootings, school shootings, "defund the police," "soft-on-crime," and gun legislation debates. Fifty-one years since its founding, the Congressional Black Caucus **(See #77)** - which now includes Representatives Maxine Waters, Sheila Jackson Lee, Barbara Lee, Al Green, Ayanna Pressley, Cori Bush, Frederica Wilson, and Senators Corey Booker, Raphael Warnock, and included the late John Lewis **(See #64, #70)** - is needed now more than ever, as the most critical promises Biden campaigned on and promised to Black voters remain in limbo or dead on a congressional floor, yet to be revived. At the time of this book's publication, the following issues are still pending. **Voter Access: The John R. Lewis Voting Rights Advancement Act and Freedom to Vote Act** to counteract state- led efforts to limit or scrutinize minority voting. **Still Pending**. Despite Thurgood Marshall's triumphant victory in

*Smith v. Allwright* 78 years before **(See #55)**, both red and blue states are still gerrymandering and redistricting voting lines which structurally suppresses the Black vote, guarantees unopposed congressional victories in some cases and hinders democracy overall. [480][481][482][483] **Policing: The George Floyd Policing Act** to improve police training, invest in community programs, combat police misconduct, like excessive force choke holds and carotid holds, and end racial bias in policing. **Still Pending. The Wealth Gap:** There is a $153,000 gap in median net worth between Blacks and Whites. Additionally, Blacks are twice as likely to be unemployed, and student loan debt repayment affects Black borrowers significantly more due to the disproportionate income and wealth gaps. **Still Pending.** [484] **Farming Distribution:** After years of discrimination, land theft, and loan rejections, Black farmers face foreclosures and have yet to see the financial relief promised to them as White farmers, who have received monetary compensation. **Still Pending.** [485][486] **Home Ownership:** Blacks still face predatory loans, making them more vulnerable to foreclosures, and often pay higher mortgage fees and receive lower appraisals than White owners, buyers, and sellers. [487] **School Education:** While all of this is going on, the United Daughters of Confederacy textbook revolution has returned as states, school districts, teachers, and parents argue vehemently over **Critical Race**

Theory (See #81) [488] and whether Black History lessons should be taught in schools. *Dictionary Sidenote: Critical Race Theory is an academic concept that is more than 40 years old. The core idea is that race is a social construct and that racism is not merely the product of individual bias or prejudice but also something embedded in legal systems and policies. The problem is not bad people but a system that reproduces bad outcomes. One example we have already discussed which would fall in this category is racially restrictive covenants, a terribly flawed system with egregiously bad outcomes for Black people; no homes, thus no real opportunity to build wealth.* Certain districts are banning a long list of books, and governors are attempting to make Black History optional or implement policies that will ban subjects if it makes White students feel bad, ashamed, or guilty for past occurrences. [489] [490] *No one ever asks the Black and Brown kids how they feel about not seeing themselves in history books. And I imagine this book would most certainly and very quickly be banned from certain schools and thrown in a Christian Tennessee fire.* Despite all the pending, there is some acknowledgment of the failings and criticisms. Biden pledges to nominate a Black woman to the Supreme Court after Justice Stephen Breyer retires. [491] But polls continue to show Black America is less satisfied with Biden and the country's direction. Stats such as this strike fear in Democrats as midterms and presidential elections approach. [492] [493] *Although the supreme court nomination is huge, it wasn't among the list of priority requests made by 92% of the Black voting constituents. The question and concern are not necessarily whether the Black voting bloc will choose the other guy or gal, but whether they will even show up to vote at all, after finally being fed up with being told "to be patient" and realizing their grievances and concerns seem to always get pushed to the back.*

## 100. Here's to Getting it Right... Hopefully.

Congress can't pass anything else Blacks specifically requested but hey, at least Juneteenth is finally passed as a federal holiday, and we've got an alternative BBQ day! [494] Fifty-six years after the assassination of Malcolm X, Norman 3X Butler (now Muhammad Aziz) and Thomas 15X Johnson (now Khalil Islam and deceased) **(See #70)** are exonerated based on "newly discovered evidence." The evidence was (1) A description of the killers that did not match Aziz or Islam, (2) An admission that the only witnesses who fingered Aziz and Islam were FBI informants operating under the orders of FBI Director Hoover **(See #63)**, and (3) A report that said photos of Islam had failed to place him in the Audubon Ballroom where Malcolm X was assassinated on Feb. 21, 1965. *Remember Talmadge Hayer told the courts these men were not involved, yet they were found guilty. Ironic how the system always finds its "guilty button" when the perpetrator is of a darker hue.* The same league that ousted Colin Kaepernick is again reeling in scandal as it's currently reviewing its **"Rooney Rule"** and hiring practices of Black and minority head coaches. *The Rooney Rule is an NFL policy* *that requires teams to interview minority candidates for head coaching positions. Not so fun fact: There were more Black head coaches before the Rooney Rule was invented in 2003 than there are today. At the time of this book, there are only two Black head coaches.* There have been more than 200 mass shootings, and gun debates are back on the congressional docket. Across the Atlantic pond, the world is watching Russia invade Ukraine, albeit terribly. And while many support one side of the war, financially or with material support, Black soldiers are waiting and wondering if they will be called on, yet again, to join another fight for... freedom? **(See #9, #19, #28, #31, #39, #44, #54, #58, #61, #84, #87).** Additionally, Black America is also wondering how the government can provide trillions to one European country under attack and at the same time proclaim empty pockets when it comes to their issues. *Quite possibly another contributing reason why Black America is less satisfied with the Biden-Harris administration.* But on a brighter note and to close out 2022 Black History Month, President Biden keeps his Supreme Court promise and nominates Ketanji Brown Jackson as the next Chief Justice and the first Black woman to receive the honor in the 233-year history of the Supreme Court. She is the same vice chair who helped change the sentencing guidelines for the crack-cocaine disparity that disproportionately harmed Black and Brown communities **(See #90)**. [495] [496] Finally, on March 7, 57 years after "Bloody Sunday" **(See #70)**, 107 years after the "first" recorded lynching **(See #22)**, 187 years after the Dyer Anti-Lynching Bill attempt **(See #46)**, and two years after the stalled Emmett Till Anti-Lynching Bill attempt, the House and the Senate pass the first-ever federal anti-lynching bill. [497] The bill imposes criminal penalties, fines, and imprisonment, on an individual who conspires to commit a hate crime offense that results in death or serious bodily injury. [498] Exactly one month later, Congress votes and confirms Judge Ketanji Brown Jackson as the newest member of the Supreme Court. [499][500] In 233 years, there have been 115 sitting justices. Only five have been women, the first being Sandra Day O' Connor in 1981, followed by Ruth Bader Ginsburg, Sonia Sotomayor, Elena Kagan, and Amy Coney Barrett. Two justices have been Black— Thurgood Marshall and Clarence Thomas. That's 108 White men ranging from slave-owning racists to conservative and progressives shaping the entirety of American history. And now, for the first time since 1789 **(See #12)**, a Black woman joins the list of Supreme Court justices. America, the land of celebrated first, but here's to progress and getting it right... hopefully.

*****

*"History, as nearly no one seems to know, is not merely something to be read. And it does not refer merely, or even principally, to the past. On the contrary, the great force of history comes from the fact that we carry it within us, are unconsciously controlled by it in many ways, and history is literally present in all that we do. It could scarcely be otherwise since it is to history that we owe our frames of reference, our identities, and our aspirations."*
*- James Baldwin*

# THE OUTRO:

## OF ELEPHANTS OR MICE

1526-2022. 496 years of Black enslavement, tragedy, oppression, strategic ruin, courage, bravery, sacrifice, genius, invention, culture, triumph, dignity, resiliency, and enduring spirit. 496 years of trying to prove to an entire country that you are human and deserving of equal treatment. 496 years and still asking:

**How much have things really changed?**
**How much have they remained the same?**

Dr. Martin Luther King would not see his "American Dream" come to pass. In fact, if the 93-year-old King were still alive today, he would still be waiting. There are many challenges and roadblocks which continue to affect us today. In many ways, racial segregation and discrimination in America has worsened, sustaining the illusion of progress, and masking a reality of continued systemic oppression. The Civil Rights Acts of the mid-'50s and '60s were monumental moments that signaled an end to discrimination on paper but unfortunately lacked the enforcement powers and support at the local and state levels leaving many issues unchanged. And even after those laws passed, protests continued because of the realization that congressional bills provide little to nothing by themselves. They need a body politic that actually believes in them.

**This is who we are, but it's not who we have to be.**

And so the fight that has been ongoing since 1526 and 1865 continues, but when will the fight begin for you? For the dignity, self-worth, and realistic potential of equal opportunity across the board, regardless of race? For quality education and true citizenship directly tied to the equal access and opportunity of a good job, a decent living wage, affordable housing, and the right to healthcare and nourishment? When will the fight for a real American Dream begin? On paper and in practice. One that is not tied to wealth and material success but is deeply entrenched in the intrinsic health of the people who make this nation what it is and what it can be.

**You and Me.**

The dreams of our heroes, sheroes, and inspirational leaders did not die in an Audubon Ballroom, on a balcony in Memphis, on a street in Oakland, or in a nursing home in Mexico. Instead, that was the day it began with us.

And as we find ourselves in truly historical times, we must ask ourselves, individually and collectively, what will the soul of this country become? If not for ourselves, then for our children and their children. Because just as most of us have grown up with the stories of the movements of the 1950s and 1960s, our next generations will research what happened in 2008 and, especially beyond 2020.

We must seek to challenge ourselves to be better going forward, understand more, find empathy, listen before critique, and simply be open-minded enough to have the "tough" conversations. No matter how difficult they are, conversations alone have never held us back or created "more division." Does it mean we all get along and agree? Absolutely not. The best of us found difficulties in getting along with the ideologies of others, and some even remained at odds throughout their lifetimes, but that never deterred them from the ultimate goal. The differences are okay so long as they don't end in stalemate and the results remain mutually understood and accepted.

What will hold us back is the unwillingness to be better than who we are, but only through history can we see exactly who we have been to be something different, good, and humane. How else do we progress as a society and as a nation of citizens, neighbors, and coworkers without discussing societal failures, tragedies, victories, and progress within a manner of respectable discourse? Hiding, being shunned, or being too afraid to engage on certain topics only magnifies our confusion and misunderstandings and dissuades empathy for those who need it most - simply because we have been too afraid or too angry or too trepidatious to ask our questions.

**Our problems have always been the elephant in the room because we've been too afraid to turn it into a mouse for far too long.**

Yes, it will be exhausting. It will be tiresome. It will be overwhelming—emotionally, spiritually, and physically—but our history, present, and future depend on us getting it right.

Which began with you opening this book.

I sincerely hope you enjoyed it. I hope you learned. And I hope you grow. And I hope you pass on this knowledge for the sake of progress—civil, social, and otherwise—for both you and me. Thank you for choosing to be on the right side of history. It's needed more than ever.

**Marquis D. Bynum**

# THE BLACK LIST
# 1526 - 2022

# Literature and Source Material

## Recommended Literature:
1. 12 Years a Slave – Solomon Northup
2. 100 Amazing Facts About the Negro - Henry Louis Gates
3. The Autobiography of Martin Luther King, Jr - Edited by Clayborn Carson
4. The Autobiography of Malcolm X – Alex Haley
5. Black Skin, White Masks – Franz Fanon
6. By Any Means Necessary – Malcolm X
7. The Color of Law - Richard Rothstein
8. The Destruction of the Black Civilization – Chancellor Williams

9. The Fiery Trial: Abraham Lincoln and American Slavery – Eric Foner
10. The Fire Next Time – James Baldwin
11. Frederick Douglass, Prophet of Freedom – David Blight
12. Gateway to Freedom – Eric Foner
13. The Half Has Never Been Told – Edward Baptist
14. I Am Not Your Negro – James Baldwin
15. The Immortal Life of Henrietta Lacks – Rebecca Skloot
16. Incidents in the Life of a Slave Girl – Harriet Jacobs
17. The Interesting Narrative of the Life of Olaudah Equiano - Olaudah Equiano
18. The Isis Papers – Dr. Frances Cress Welsing
19. Life Upon These Shores - Henry Louis Gates
20. The Movements of the New Left: 1950-1975 – Van Gosse
21. The New Jim Crow - Michelle Alexander
22. A People's History of The United States - Howard Zinn
23. Race and Reunion: The Civil War in American Memory – David Blight
24. Revolutionary Suicide – Huey P. Newton
25. Stamped from the Beginning – Ibram X. Kendi
26. The Slave Ship – Marcus Rediker
27. Slavery by Another Name – Douglas Blackmon

# A Must Read:

The Case for Reparations, By Ta-Nehisi Coates - https://www.theatlantic.com/magazine/archive/201 4/06/the-case-for-reparations/361631/

# Web Sites (In Chronological Order):

[1] The Forgotten First Attempt To Plant A Colony On US Soil - https://historynewsnetwork.org/article/164750

[2] Before 1619, There Was 1526: The Mystery Of The First Enslaved Africans In What Became The United States - https://www.washingtonpost.com/history/2019/09/07/before-there-was-mystery-first-enslaved-africans-what-became-us/

[3] America's History Of Slavery Began Long Before Jamestown - https://www.history.com/news/american-slavery-before-jamestown-1619

[4] The Misguided Focus On 1619 As The Beginning Of Slavery In The U.S. Damages Our Understanding Of American History - https://www.smithsonianmag.com/history/misguided-focus-1619-beginning-slavery-us-damages-our-understanding-american-history-180964873/

[5] First Enslaved Africans Arrive In Jamestown, Setting The Stage For Slavery In North America - https://www.history.com/this-day-in-history/first-african-slave-ship-arrives-jamestown-colony

[6] The First Africans - https://historicjamestowne.org/history/the-first-africans/

[7] Pocahontas: Her Life And Legend - https://www.nps.gov/jame/learn/historyculture/pocahontas-her-life-and-legend.htm

[8] First Enslaved Africans Arrive In Jamestown, Setting The Stage For Slavery In North America - https://www.history.com/this-day-in-history/first-african-slave-ship-arrives-jamestown-colony

[9] The First Africans - https://historicjamestowne.org/history/the-first-africans/

[10] John Punch -
https://www.thirteen.org/wnet/slavery/experience/responses/spotlight.html

[11] Slavery And The Making Of America -
https://www.thirteen.org/wnet/slavery/timeline/1619.html

[12] Elizabeth Key -
https://www.lva.virginia.gov/public/dvb/bio.php?b=key_elizabeth_fl_1655-1660

[13] Slavery And The Making Of America -
https://www.thirteen.org/wnet/slavery/timeline/1662.html#:~:text=slavery%20and%20the%20making%20of,timeline%20%7c%20pbs&text=virginia%20enacts%20a%20law%20of,mother%20inherits%20her%20slave%20status.&text=massachusetts%20reverses%20a%20ruling%20dating,blacks%20to%20train%20in%20arms

[14] Virginia Slave Laws -
http://www.digitalhistory.uh.edu/disp_textbook.cfm?smtid=3&psid=71

[15] The Hidden History Of Slavery In New York -
https://www.thenation.com/article/archive/hidden-history-slavery-new-york/

[16] History Of Slavery In New York -
http://www.slaveryinnewyork.org/history.htm

[17] Slavery In America - https://www.history.com/topics/black-history/slavery

[18] Slavery In America (Timeline) - https://www.ferris.edu/htmls/news/jimcrow/timeline/slavery.htm

[19] Slavery In America: The Montgomery Slave Trade - https://eji.org/reports/slavery-in-america/

[20] 400 Years Since Slavery - https://www.theguardian.com/news/2019/aug/15/400-years-since-slavery-timeline

[21] Slave Patrols: An Early Form Of American Policing - https://lawenforcementmuseum.org/2019/07/10/slave-patrols-an-early-form-of-american-policing/

[22] How An African Slave Helped Boston Fight Smallpox - https://www.bostonglobe.com/ideas/2014/10/17/how-african-slave-helped-boston-fight-smallpox/xfhsmmvtgcev62yp0xhhzi/story.html

[23] The Slave Who Helped Boston Battle Smallpox - https://undark.org/2020/04/02/slave-smallpox-onesimus/

[24] The Stono Rebellion - https://www.pbs.org/wgbh/aia/part1/1p284.html

[25] The Stono Rebellion - https://billofrightsinstitute.org/essays/the-stono-rebellion

[26] Stono Rebellion - https://www.loc.gov/item/today-in-history/september-09/

[27] The Negro Act – https://calendar.eji.org/racial-injustice/may/10

[28] Phillis Wheatley –
http://www.americaslibrary.gov/jb/revolut/jb_revolut_poetslav_1.html

[29] 7 Black Heroes Of The American Revolution -
https://www.history.com/news/black-heroes-american-revolution#:~:text=historians%20estimate%20that%20between%20 5%2c000,lost%20to%20our%20collective%20memory

[30] The Revolutionary War -
https://www.pbs.org/wgbh/aia/part2/2narr4.html

[31] Dec Of Independence - The Right To Vote ONLY For Men With Property -
https://www.loc.gov/teachers/classroommaterials/presentationsandactivities/presentations/elections/founders-and-the-vote.html

[32] Is The Declaration Of Independence Based On A Lie? -
https://www.forbes.com/sites/tomlindsay/2016/06/30/is-the-- declaration-of-independence-based-on-a-lie/#2a7c3be66774

[33] Vermont 1777: Early Steps Against Slavery -
https://nmaahc.si.edu/explore/stories/vermont-1777-early-steps-against-slavery

[34] Quakers (Society Of Friends) -
http://abolition.e2bn.org/people_21.html

[35] Quakers: From Slave Traders To Early Abolitionists -
https://www.pbs.org/thisfarbyfaith/journey_1/p_7.html#:~:text=the%20quakers%20were%20among%20the,their%20fight%20began%20in%20pennsylvania

[36] Underground Railroad -
https://www.history.com/topics/black-history/underground-railroad

[37] Before There Were "Red" And "Blue" States, There Were "Free" States And "Slave" States -
https://law.marquette.edu/facultyblog/2012/12/before-there-were-red-and-blue-states-there-were-free-states-and-slave-states/#:~:text=in%201780%2c%20pennsylvania%20became%20the,by%20judicial%20decree%20in%201783

[38] Congress Enacts the Northwest Ordinance -
https://www.history.com/this-day-in-history/congress-enacts-the-northwest-ordinance

[39] The Life Of Sally Hemings -
https://www.monticello.org/sallyhemings/

[40] Three-Fifths Compromise -
https://www.britannica.com/topic/three-fifths-compromise

[41] 1790 U.S. Census -
https://www.census.gov/history/www/through_the_decades/overview/1790.html

[42] Did Slaves Build The White House (From White House Itself) –
https://www.whitehousehistory.org/questions/did-slaves-build-the-white-house

[43] The White House Was In Fact Built By Slaves
https://www.smithsonianmag.com/smart-news/white-house-was-fact-built-slaves-180959916/

[44] 15 American Landmarks Built By Slaves -
https://www.businessinsider.com/american-landmarks-that-were-built-by-slaves-2019-9

[45] Benjamin Banneker -
https://www.whitehousehistory.org/benjamin-banneker

[46] 15 American Landmarks That Were Built By Slaves -
https://www.businessinsider.com/american-landmarks-that-were-built-by-slaves-2019-9

[47] Fugitive Slave Act -
https://www.battlefields.org/learn/primary-sources/fugitive-slave-act#:~:text=passed%20on%20september%2018%2c%201850,return i ng%2c%20and%20trying%20escaped%20slaves

[48] Fugitive Slave Acts - https://www.history.com/topics/black-history/fugitive-slave-acts

[49] Solomon Northup – https://freedomcenter.org/journey-to-freedom/about-solomon-northup

[50] Twelve Years A Slave: Narrative Of Solomon Northup, A Citizen Of New York Kidnapped In Washington City In 1841, And Rescued In 1853 -
https://docsouth.unc.edu/fpn/northup/northup.html

[51] Watch: "12 Years A Slave." (2013). Directed By Steve Mcqueen. Starring Chiwetel Ejiofor, Michael Fassbender, Lupita Nyong'o and Brad Pitt

[52] Eli Whitney And Cotton Gin (Slave Boom) -
https://www.history.com/topics/inventions/cotton-gin-and-eli-whitney

[53] Oney Judge -
https://www.mountvernon.org/library/digitalhistory/digital - encyclopedia/article/ona-judge

[54] George Washington And The Slave Who Got Away (Oney Judge) - https://www.history.com/news/george-washington-and-the-slave-who-got-away

[55] Jean-Baptiste Point Dusable (1745-1818) - https://www.blackpast.org/african-american-history/dusable-jean-baptiste-point-1745-1818/

[56] Gabriel's Conspiracy, Encyclopedia Virginia - https://encyclopediavirginia.org/entries/gabriels-conspiracy-1800/

[57] What Is The Electoral College? Library Of Congress - https://www.loc.gov/classroom-materials/elections/presidential-election-process/what-is-the-electoral-college/

[58] What Is The Electoral College? National Archives - https://www.archives.gov/electoral-college/about

[59] Why Bibles Given To Slaves Omitted Most Of The Old Testament - https://www.history.com/news/slave-bible-redacted-old-testament

[60] Slave Bible From The 1800s Omitted Key Passages That Could Incite Rebellion - https://www.npr.org/2018/12/09/674995075/slave-bible-from-the-1800s-omitted-key-passages-that-could-incite-rebellion

[61] Congress Abolishes The African Slave Trade - https://www.history.com/this-day-in-history/congress-abolishes-the-african-slave-trade

[62] End Of Slave Trade Meant New Normal For America – https://www.npr.org/templates/story/story.php?storyid=17988106

[63] The War Of 1812 - https://www.history.com/topics/war-of-1812/war-of-1812

[64] A Brief Overview Of The War Of 1812 - https://www.battlefields.org/learn/articles/brief-overview-war-1812

[65] African Americans And The War Of 1812: A Lightning Lesson From Teaching With Historic Places - https://www.nps.gov/subjects/warof1812/african-american-story.htm

[66] History Of Fort Mchenry - https://www.nps.gov/fomc/learn/historyculture/history-of-fort-mchenry.htm

[67] Grace Wisher - https://www.nps.gov/fomc/learn/historyculture/grace-wisher.htm

[68] Star-Spangled Banner Official - https://www.history.com/this-day-in-history/the-star-spangled-banner-becomes-official

[69] Complete Version Of The US National Anthem, The Star-Spangled Banner - https://amhistory.si.edu/starspangledbanner/pdf/ssb_lyrics.pdf

[70] American Colonization Society - https://www.blackpast.org/african-american-history/american-colonization-society-1816-1964/

[71] How A Movement To Send Freed Slaves To Africa Created Liberia - https://www.history.com/news/slavery-american-colonization-society-liberia

[72] Denmark Vessey - https://www.nps.gov/people/denmark-vesey.htm

[73] Nat Turner - https://www.britannica.com/biography/nat-turner

[74] Before Central Park: The Story Of Seneca Village - https://www.centralparknyc.org/articles/seneca-village

[75] The Life Of Sally Hemings - https://www.monticello.org/sallyhemings/

[76] Negative Racial Stereotypes And Their Effect On Attitudes Toward African Americans - https://www.ferris.edu/htmls/news/jimcrow/links/essays/vcu.htm

[77] Thomas Rice - https://exhibits.lib.usf.edu/exhibits/show/minstrelsy/jimcrow-to-jolson/jump-jim-crow

[78] Minstrel Shows - https://www.britannica.com/art/minstrel-show#ref1067215

[79] The Origins Of Jim Crow - https://www.ferris.edu/htmls/news/jimcrow/origins.htm

[80] Phrenology And "Scientific Racism" In The 19th Century - https://pages.vassar.edu/realarchaeology/2017/03/05/phrenology-and-scientific-racism-in-the-19th-century/

[81] Django Unchained And The Racist Science Of Phrenology - https://www.theguardian.com/science/blog/2013/feb/05/django-unchained-racist-science-phrenology

[82] Watch – Django Unchained, Scene: Calvin Candie, Phrenology And "Old Ben's" Skull. Directed By Quentin Tarantino And Starring Leonardo Dicaprio, Jamie Foxx, Christoph Waltz, Samuel L. Jackson And Kerry Washington

[83] The History Of Policing - https://plsonline.eku.edu/insidelook/history-policing-united - states-part-1

[84] How The U.S. Got Its Police Force - https://time.com/4779112/police-history-origins/

[85] History Of Policing And Race In The US Are Deeply Intertwined - https://www.npr.org/2020/06/13/876628302/the-history-of-policing-and-race-in-the-u-s-are-deeply-intertwined

[86] Frederick Douglass - https://www.nps.gov/frdo/learn/historyculture/frederickdougl ass.htm

[87] The Great Escape From Slavery of Ellen and William Craft - https://www.smithsonianmag.com/history/the-great-escape-from-slavery-of-ellen-and-william-craft-497960/

[88] Harriet Tubman - https://www.nps.gov/people/harriet-tubman.htm

[89] People & Events: Harriet Tubman - https://www.pbs.org/wgbh/aia/part4/4p1535.html

[90] Jack Daniel, Our Story - https://www.jackdaniels.com/en-us/our-story

[91] Henry "Box" Brown - https://www.pbs.org/black-culture/shows/list/underground-railroad/stories-freedom/henry-box-brown/

[92] Drapetomania - https://www.ferris.edu/htmls/news/jimcrow/question/2005/n ovember.htm

[93] The Fugitive Slave Acts Of 1793 And 1850 - http://www.math.buffalo.edu/~sww/0history/slaveacts.html

[94] Sojourner Truth: Ain't I A Woman? - https://www.nps.gov/articles/sojourner-truth.htm

[95] The Tom Caricature - https://www.ferris.edu/htmls/news/jimcrow/tom/homepage.htm

[96] Why African Americans Loathe 'Uncle Tom' - https://www.npr.org/templates/story/story.php?storyid=93059468

[97] A Nation's Story: "What To The Slave Is The Fourth Of July?" - https://nmaahc.si.edu/blog-post/nations-story-%e2%80%9cwhat-slave-fourth-july%e2%80%9d

[98] Martin R. Delany (1812-1885) - https://encyclopediavirginia.org/entries/delany-martin-r-1812-1885/

[99] Dred Scott V. Sanford (Actual Law) - https://www.oyez.org/cases/1850-1900/60us393

[100] Dred Scott V. Sanford (History) - https://www.history.com/topics/black-history/dred-scott-case

[101] How Slavery Became America's First Big Business - https://www.vox.com/identities/2019/8/16/20806069/slavery-economy-capitalism-violence-cotton-edward-baptist

[102] How Slavery Became The Economic Engine Of The South - https://www.history.com/news/slavery-profitable-southern-economy

[103] Slavery Made America - https://www.theatlantic.com/business/archive/2014/06/slavery-made-america/373288/

[104] The Clear Connection Between Slavery And American Capitalism -

https://www.forbes.com/sites/hbsworkingknowledge/2017/05/03/the-clear-connection-between-slavery-and-american-capitalism/#13a754147bd3

[105] Lincoln-Douglas Debates - https://www.history.com/topics/19th-century/lincoln-douglas-debates

[106] The Lincoln-Douglas Debates 4th Debate Part I, By Abraham Lincoln & Stephen A. Douglas - https://teachingamericanhistory.org/document/the-lincoln-douglas-debates-4th-debate-part-i/

[107] Confederate States Of America - https://www.history.com/topics/american-civil-war/confederate-states-of-america

[108] CSA Constitution - https://avalon.law.yale.edu/19th_century/csa_csa.asp

[109] Fort Sumter - https://www.battlefields.org/learn/civil-war/battles/fort-sumter

[110] The Civil War – Causes, Dates And Battles - https://www.history.com/topics/american-civil-war/american-civil-war-history

[111] A Revolution in Haiti - http://scholar.library.miami.edu/slaves/san_domingo_revolution/individual_essay/jason.html

[112] The United States and the Haitian Revolution, 1791–1804 - https://history.state.gov/milestones/1784-1800/haitian-rev

[113] Outnumbered Mexican Army Defeats French At Battle Of Puebla - https://www.history.com/this-day-in-history/cinco-de-mayo

[114] Black Civil War Soldiers - https://www.history.com/topics/american-civil-war/black-civil-war-soldiers

[115] Black Troops In Union Blue - https://www.crf-usa.org/black-history-month/black-troops-in-union-blue

[116] The 54th Massachusetts Regiment - https://www.nps.gov/articles/54th-massachusetts-regiment.htm

[117] Watch: Glory (1989). Directed By Edward Zwick. Starring Matthew Broderick, Denzel Washington, Cary Elwes And Morgan Freeman

[118] Robert Smalls - https://www.pbs.org/wnet/african-americans-many-rivers-to-cross/history/which-slave-sailed-himself-to-freedom/

[119] Cathay Williams - https://www.nps.gov/people/cwilliams.htm

[120] Ida B. Wells - https://www.nps.gov/people/idabwells.htm

[121] Lincoln's Evolving Thoughts On Slavery, And Freedom - https://www.npr.org/2010/10/11/130489804/lincolns-evolving-thoughts-on-slavery-and-freedom

[122] 5 Things You May Not Know About Abraham Lincoln, Slavery And Emancipation - https://www.history.com/news/5-things-you-may-not-know-about-lincoln-slavery-and-emancipation

[123] The Emancipation Proclamation - https://www.archives.gov/exhibits/featured-documents/emancipation-proclamation#:~:text=president%20abraham%20lincoln%20issued%20the,and%20henceforward%20shall%20be%20free.%22

[124] The Emancipation Proclamation, History - https://www.history.com/topics/american-civil-war/emancipation-proclamation

[125] How Jack Daniel Came To Make Whiskey - https://www.jackdaniels.com/en-us/vault/how-jack-daniel-came-make-whiskey

[126] About Nearest Green - http://nearestgreen.org/about-nearest-green/

[127] Sherman's Field Order No. 15 - https://www.georgiaencyclopedia.org/articles/history-archaeology/shermans-field-order-no-15/

[128] (1865) General William T. Sherman's Special Field Order No. 15 - https://www.blackpast.org/african-american-history/special-field-orders-no-15/

[129] Dr. Booker Taliaferro Washington - https://www.tuskegee.edu/discover-tu/tu-presidents/booker-t-washington

[130] The Civil War, 4 Million Freed. 750,000 Dead. 1 Nation Saved - https://www.nps.gov/civilwar/index.htm

[131] Juneteenth - https://www.pbs.org/wnet/african-americans-many-rivers-to-cross/history/what-is-juneteenth/

[132] The American West, 1865-1900 - https://www.loc.gov/classroom-materials/united-states-history-primary-source-timeline/rise-of-industrial-america-1876-1900/american-west-1865-1900/

[133] Westward Expansion -
https://www.history.com/topics/westward-expansion/westward-expansion

[134] Buffalo Soldiers & Indian Wars -
https://www.buffalosoldier.net/

[135] The Myth Of The Buffalo Soldiers -
https://www.blackpast.org/african-american-history/myth-buffalo-soldiers/

[136] Civil Rights in America: Racial Voting Rights -
https://www.nps.gov/subjects/tellingallamericansstories/upload/civilrights_votingrights.pdf

[137] The Lost Cause: A New Southern History Of The War Of The Confederates By Edward Pollard -
https://thereconstructionera.com/the-lost-cause-a-new-southern-history-of-the-war-of-the-confederates-by-edward-pollard/

[138] The Lost Cause -
https://encyclopediavirginia.org/entries/lost-cause-the/

[139] Reconstruction - https://www.history.com/topics/american-civil-war/reconstruction

[140] The Travails Of Reconstruction -
https://www.loc.gov/classroom-materials/united-states-history-primary-source-timeline/civil-war-and-reconstruction-1861-1877/travails-of-reconstruction/

[141] Black Codes - https://www.history.com/topics/black-history/black-codes

[142] Black Codes And Pig Laws -
https://www.pbs.org/tpt/slavery-by-another-name/themes/black-codes/

[143] The Black Codes And Jim Crow Laws -
https://www.nationalgeographic.org/encyclopedia/black-codes
- and-jim-crow-laws/

[144] Southern Black Codes - https://www.crf-usa.org/brown-v-
board-50th-anniversary/southern-black-codes.html

[145] The Freedmen's Bureau -
https://www.archives.gov/research/african-
americans/freedmens-bureau

[146] Sharecropping - https://www.pbs.org/tpt/slavery-by-
another-
name/themes/sharecropping/#:~:text=sharecropping%20is%20a
%20system%20where,to%20leave%20for%20other%20opportunit
i es

[147] Vagrancy Act Of 1866 -
https://www.encyclopediavirginia.org/vagrancy_act_of_1866

[148] Convict Leasing - https://www.thoughtco.com/convict-
leasing-4160457

[149] Convict Lease System -
http://www.digitalhistory.uh.edu/disp_textbook.cfm?smtid=2&
psid=3179

[150] Convict Leasing - https://www.pbs.org/tpt/slavery-by-
another-name/themes/convict-leasing/

[151] Watch: "13th" Netflix Original Documentary (2016). Directed By
Ava Duvernay

[152] Grant, Reconstruction And The KKK -
https://www.pbs.org/wgbh/americanexperience/features/grant
-kkk/

[153] Ku Klux Klan (History) -
https://www.history.com/topics/reconstruction/ku-klux-klan

[154] History Of The KKK In Georgia From 1868-1944 -
https://www.arcgis.com/apps/cascade/index.html?appid=0f3a7
e1ce9094014b64456b322854404

[155] Landmark Legislation: Thirteenth, Fourteenth, & Fifteenth
Amendments -
https://www.senate.gov/artandhistory/history/common/generi
c/civilwaramendments.htm

[156] John Willis Menard - https://history.house.gov/historical-
highlights/1851-1900/john-willis-menard-of-louisiana-became-
the-first-african-american-to-address-the-u-s--house/

[157] First College To Admit Blacks -
https://www.ferris.edu/htmls/news/jimcrow/question/2010/ju
ne.htm

[158] Key Events In Black Higher Education -
https://www.jbhe.com/chronology/

[159] Landmark Legislation: Thirteenth, Fourteenth, & Fifteenth
Amendments -
https://www.senate.gov/artandhistory/history/common/generi
c/civilwaramendments.htm

[160] Grant, Reconstruction And The KKK -
https://www.pbs.org/wgbh/americanexperience/features/grant
-kkk/

[161] Black Americans In Congress: An Introduction -
https://history.house.gov/exhibitions-and-
publications/baic/historical-essays/introduction/introduction/

[162] Civil Rights Act Of 1875 - https://history.house.gov/historical-
highlights/1851-1900/the-civil-rights-act-of-1875/

[163] About The US Civil Rights Act Of 1875 -
https://www.thoughtco.com/civil-rights-act-1875-412978
2

[164] Civil Rights Act Of 1875 - https://history.house.gov/historical-
highlights/1851-1900/the-civil-rights-act-of-1875/

[165] Lewis Latimer - https://lemelson.mit.edu/resources/lewis-
latimer

[166] The Black Investor, Lewis Latimer -
https://lemelson.mit.edu/resources/lewis-latimer

[167] The African Dodger -
https://www.ferris.edu/htmls/news/jimcrow/question/2012/o
ctober.htm

[168] Abolition -
https://www.nps.gov/stli/learn/historyculture/abolition.htm

[169] The Statue Of Liberty Was Created To Celebrate Freed Slaves,
Not Immigrants, Its New Museum Recounts -
https://www.washingtonpost.com/history/2019/05/23/statue-
liberty-was-created-celebrate-freed-slaves-not-immigrants/

[170] How Jim Crow-Era Laws Suppressed the African American
Vote for Generations - https://www.history.com/news/jim-
crow-laws-black-vote

[171] Civil Rights in America: Racial Voting Rights -
https://www.nps.gov/subjects/tellingallamericansstories/uploa
d/civilrights_votingrights.pdf

[172] The 'Mississippi Plan' to keep Blacks from voting in 1890: 'We
came here to exclude the Negro' -
https://www.washingtonpost.com/history/2021/05/01/mississ
i ppi-constitution-voting-rights-jim-crow/

[173] Voting Rights Discrimination - https://www.crf-usa.org/black-history-month/race-and-voting-in-the-segregated-south

[174] Today Is National Voter Registration Day. The Evolution Of American Voting Rights In 242 Years Shows How Far We've Come — And How Far We Still Have To Go - https://www.businessinsider.com/when-women-got-the-right-to-vote-american-voting-rights-timeline-2018-10

[175] The Racial History Of The 'Grandfather Clause' - https://www.npr.org/sections/codeswitch/2013/10/21/239081586/the-racial-history-of-the-grandfather-clause

[176] Plessy V. Ferguson (Law) - https://www.oyez.org/cases/1850-1900/163us537

[177] Plessy V. Ferguson (History) - https://www.history.com/topics/black-history/plessy-v-ferguson

[178] The Great Migration (1910-1970) - https://www.archives.gov/research/african-americans/migrations/great-migration

[179] The Long-Lasting Legacy Of The Great Migration - https://www.smithsonianmag.com/history/long-lasting-legacy-great-migration-180960118/

[180] Sundown Towns: A Hidden Dimension Of American Racism - https://www.zinnedproject.org/materials/sundown-towns/

[181] Alphabetical Map Of Sundown Towns By State - https://justice.tougaloo.edu/sundown-towns/using-the-sundown-towns-database/state-map/

[182] W.E.B. Du Bois - https://hutchinscenter.fas.harvard.edu/web-dubois

[183] Buffalo Soldiers And The Spanish-American War - https://www.nps.gov/prsf/learn/historyculture/buffalo-soldiers-and-the-spanish-american-war.htm

[184] The Lost History Of An American Coup D'Etat - https://www.theatlantic.com/politics/archive/2017/08/wilming ton-massacre/536457/

[185] Nov. 10, 1898: Wilmington Massacre - https://www.zinnedproject.org/news/tdih/wilmington-massacre-2/

[186] Ida B. Wells-Barnett, "Lynch Law In America" (1900) - https://www.americanyawp.com/reader/18-industrial-america/ida-b-wells-barnett-lynch-law-in-america-1900/

[187] James Weldon Johnson - https://www.naacp.org/naacp-history-james-weldon-johnson/

[188] Lift Every Voice And Sing (Black National Anthem) - https://www.pbs.org/black-culture/explore/black-authors-spoken-word-poetry/lift-every-voice-and-sing/

[189] Booker T. Washington - https://www.history.com/topics/black-history/booker-t-washington#section_5

[190] The Souls Of Black Folk, By W.E.B. Du Bois - https://www.gutenberg.org/files/408/408-h/408-h.htm

[191] Strivings Of The Negro People - https://www.theatlantic.com/magazine/archive/1897/08/striv i ngs-of-the-negro-people/305446/

[192] The First Human Zoos - https://www.ferris.edu/htmls/news/jimcrow/question/2006/o ctober.htm

[193] Human Zoos: A Shocking History of Shame and Exploitation - https://www.cbc.ca/natureofthings/features/human-zoos-a-shocking-history-of-shame-and-exploitation

[194] The Human Zoo – Science's Dirty Secret - http://www.usd116.org/profdev/ahtc/lessons/goerssfel10/lessons/lesson3/thehumanzoo.pdf

[195] Negative Racial Stereotypes And Their Effect On Attitudes Toward African Americans - https://www.ferris.edu/htmls/news/jimcrow/links/essays/vcu.htm

[196] Overlooked No More: Nancy Green, The 'Real Aunt Jemima' - https://www.nytimes.com/2020/07/17/obituaries/nancy-green-aunt-jemima-overlooked.html

[197] Thomas Dixon, 1864-1946 And Arthur I. Keller (Arthur Ignatius), 1866-1924, The Clansman: An Historical Romance Of The Ku Klux Klan – https://docsouth.unc.edu/southlit/dixonclan/summary.html

[198] The Niagara Movement - https://www.history.com/topics/black-history/niagara-movement

[199] The Baron of Black Wall Street - https://www.forbes.com/sites/antoinegara/2020/06/18/the-bezos-of-black-wall-street-tulsa-race-riots-1921/?sh=218e0a5bf321

[200] What the Tulsa Race Massacre Destroyed - https://www.nytimes.com/interactive/2021/05/24/us/tulsa-race-massacre.html

[201] National Association Of Colored Women - http://www.crusadeforthevote.org/nacw

[202] NAACP History - https://www.naacp.org/nations-premier-civil-rights-organization/

[203] NAACP - https://www.history.com/topics/civil-rights-movement/naacp

[204] The Great Migration (1910-1970) - https://www.archives.gov/research/african-americans/migrations/great-migration#:~:text=the%20great%20migration%20was%20one,the%201910s%20until%20the%201970s

[205] The Great Migration - https://www.history.com/topics/black-history/great-migration

[206] July 4, 1910: Johnson vs Jeffries - https://www.thefightcity.com/july-4-1910-johnson-vs-jeffries-jack-johnson-james-jeffries-corbett-sullivan-tommy-burns-fight-of-the-century/

[207] The 'White Slavery' Law That Brought Down Jack Johnson is Still in Effect - https://www.history.com/news/white-slave-mann-act-jack-johnson-pardon

[208] Biography Of Harriet Tubman: Freed Enslaved People, Fought For The Union - https://www.thoughtco.com/harriet-tubman-biography-3529273

[209] The Debate Between W.E.B. Du Bois And Booker T. Washington - https://www.pbs.org/wgbh/frontline/article/debate-w-e-b-du-bois-and-booker-t-washington/

[210] "The Birth Of A Nation" Opens, Glorifying The KKK - https://www.history.com/this-day-in-history/birth-of-a-nation-opens

[211] The Influence of "The Birth of a Nation" - https://www.facinghistory.org/reconstruction-era/influence-birth-nation

[212] 100 Years Later, What's The Legacy Of 'Birth Of A Nation'? - https://www.npr.org/Sections/Codeswitch/2015/02/08/383279630/100-Years-Later-Whats-The-Legacy-Of-Birth-Of-A-Nation

[213] How Woodrow Wilson Tried To Reverse Black American Progress - https://www.history.com/news/woodrow-wilson-racial-segregation-jim-crow-ku-klux-klan

[214] The Leo Frank Case - https://www.georgiaencyclopedia.org/articles/history-archaeology/leo-frank-case/

[215] History Of The KKK In Georgia From 1868-1944 - https://www.arcgis.com/apps/cascade/index.html?appid=0f3a7e1ce9094014b64456b322854404

[216] How 'The Birth Of A Nation' Revived The Ku Klux Klan – https://www.history.com/news/kkk-birth-of-a-nation-film

[217] Ku Klux Klan (SPLC) - https://www.splcenter.org/fighting-hate/extremist-files/ideology/ku-klux-klan

[218] Ku Klux Klan (History) - https://www.history.com/topics/reconstruction/ku-klux-klan

[219] Garrett A. Morgan - http://ohiohistorycentral.org/w/garrett_a._morgan

[220] Marcus Garvey - https://www.pbs.org/wgbh/americanexperience/features/garvey-biography/

[221] Marcus Garvey And The Universal Negro Improvement Association -

http://nationalhumanitiescenter.org/tserve/twenty/tkeyinfo/ga
rvey.htm

[222] The Lost Cause's Long Legacy -
https://www.theatlantic.com/ideas/archive/2020/06/the-lost-
causes-long-legacy/613288/

[223] "Defence Of Fort Mchenry" Or "The Star-Spangled Banner,"
1814 - https://www.gilderlehrman.org/history-
resources/spotlight-primary-source/%e2%80%9cdefence-fort-
mchenry%e2%80%9d-or-%e2%80%9c-star-spangled-
banner%e2%80%9d-1814

[224] Fighting For Respect: African American Soldiers In WWI -
https://armyhistory.org/fighting-for-respect-african-american-
soldiers-in-wwi/

[225] African American Veterans Hoped Their Service In World War
I Would Secure Their Rights At Home. It Didn't -
https://time.com/5450336/african-american-veterans-wwi/

[226] The Harlem Hellfighters -
https://www.history.com/topics/world-war-i/the-harlem-
hellfighters-video

[227] One Hundred Years Ago, The Harlem Hellfighters Bravely Led
The U.S. Into WWI -
https://www.smithsonianmag.com/history/one-hundred-years-
ago-harlem-hellfighters-bravely-led-us-wwi-180968977/

[228] The African American Odyssey: A Quest For Full Citizenship -
https://www.loc.gov/exhibits/african-american-odyssey/world
- war-i-and-postwar-society.html

[229] Red Summer Of 1919 - https://www.history.com/news/red-
summer-1919-riots-chicago-dc-great-migration

[230] What Are Covenants -
https://mappingprejudice.umn.edu/what-are-covenants/

[231] Racial Covenants, A Relic Of The Past, Are Still On The Books
Across The Country -
https://www.npr.org/2021/11/17/1049052531/racial-covenants-
housing-discrimination

[232] Historical Shift From Explicit To Implicit Policies -
https://www.bostonfairhousing.org/timeline/1920s1948-
restrictive-covenants.html

[233] The Rise And Demise Of Racially Restrictive Covenants In
Bloomingdale -
https://www.dcpolicycenter.org/publications/racially-
restrictive-covenants-bloomingdale/

[234] How Southern Socialites Rewrote Civil War History: The
United Daughters Of The Confederacy Altered The South's
Memory Of The Civil War. -
https://www.vox.com/videos/2017/10/25/16545362/southern-
socialites-civil-war-history

[235] Harlem Renaissance -
https://www.history.com/topics/roaring-twenties/harlem-
renaissance

[236] A New African American Identity: The Harlem Renaissance -
https://nmaahc.si.edu/blog-post/new-african-american-identity
-harlem-renaissance

[237] Tulsa's 'Black Wall Street' Flourished As A Self-Contained Hub
In Early 1900s - https://www.history.com/news/black-wall-
street-tulsa-race-massacre

[238] The Fight To Commemorate Nancy Green, The Woman Who
Played The Original 'Aunt Jemima' -
https://www.npr.org/local/309/2020/06/19/880918717/the-

fight-to-commemorate-nancy-green-the-woman-who-played-the-original-aunt-jemima

[239] Fact Check: Aunt Jemima Model Nancy Green Didn't Create The Brand - https://www.usatoday.com/story/news/factcheck/2020/06/30/fact-check-aunt-jemima-model-didnt-create-brand-wasnt-millionaire/3241656001/

[240] Rosewood Massacre - https://www.history.com/topics/early-20th-century-us/rosewood-massacre#:~:text=the%20rosewood%20massacre%20was%20an,re sidents%20were%20driven%20out%20permanently
[241] Feb. 7, 1926: Carter G. Woodson Launched Negro History Week - https://www.zinnedproject.org/news/tdih/carter-woodson-black-history-month/

[242] The U.S. Government's Role In Sterilizing Women Of Color - https://www.thoughtco.com/u-s-governments-role-sterilizing-women-of-color-2834600

[243] The Great Depression - https://www.history.com/topics/great-depression/great-depression-history#:~:text=the%20great%20depression%20was%20the,wiped%20out%20millions%20of%20investors
[244] 9 Principal Effects Of The Great Depression - https://www.thebalance.com/effects-of-the-great-depression4049299#:~:text=the%20great%20depression%20of%201929,trade%20collapsed%2c%20and%20deflation%20soared

[245] African American Life During The Great Depression And The New Deal - https://www.britannica.com/topic/african-american/african-american-life-during-the-great-depression-and-the-new-deal

[246] Complete Version Of The US National Anthem, The Star-Spangled Banner
https://amhistory.si.edu/starspangledbanner/pdf/ssb_lyrics.pdf

[247] More Proof The U.S. National Anthem Has Always Been Tainted With Racism -
https://theintercept.com/2016/09/13/more-proof-the-u-s-national-anthem-has-always-been-tainted-with-racism/

[248] The Scottsboro Boys - https://www.thoughtco.com/timeline-of-scottsboro-boys-45428

[249] The Tuskegee Timeline (CDC) -
https://www.cdc.gov/tuskegee/timeline.htm

[250] Tuskegee Experiment: The Infamous Syphilis Study -
https://www.history.com/news/the-infamous-40-year-tuskegee-study

[251] The Mis-Education Of The Negro, By Carter Godwin Woodson, Ph.D. - http://www.jpanafrican.org/ebooks/3.4ebookthe%20mis-education.pdf

[252] Elijah Muhammad, The Leader Of The Nation Of Islam -
https://www.thoughtco.com/elijah-muhammad-leader-of-nation-of-islam-45450

[253] Federal Housing Administration (Boston Case Study) –
https://www.bostonfairhousing.org/timeline/1934-fha.html

[254] A 'Forgotten History' Of How The U.S. Government Segregated America - https://www.npr.org/2017/05/03/526655831/a-forgotten-history-of-how-the-u-s-government-segregated-america

[255] The History Of Redlining -
https://www.thoughtco.com/redlining-definition-4157858

[256] Mapping Inequality -
https://dsl.richmond.edu/panorama/redlining/#loc=5/39.1/-94.58

[257] HOLC "Redlining" Maps: The Persistent Structure Of
Segregation And Economic Inequality - https://ncrc.org/holc/

[258] When They Steal Your Land, They Steal Your Future' -
https://www.latimes.com/archives/la-xpm-2001-dec-02-mn
- 10514-story.html

[259] White Flight (New Orleans Case Study) -
http://www.datacenterresearch.org/pre-
katrina/tertiary/white.html

[260] White Flight Alive And Well -
https://www.theatlantic.com/business/archive/2015/07/white-
flight-alive-and-well/399980/

[261] The Negro Motorist Green Book -
https://www.blackpast.org/african-american-history/negro-
motorist-green-book-1936-
1964/#:~:text=the%20negro%20motorist%20green%20book%2c%
2
0popularly%20known%20as%20the%20green,would%20accept%2
0african%20american%20customers

[262] The Real Green Book -
https://www.theatlantic.com/entertainment/archive/2019/02/r
eal-green-book-preserving-stories-of-jim-crow-era-travel/583294/

[263] Pauli Murray's Indelible Mark On The Fight For Equal Rights -
https://www.aclu.org/issues/womens-rights/pauli-murrays-
indelible-mark-fight-equal-rights

[264] Congress Of Racial Equality (CORE) -
https://kinginstitute.stanford.edu/encyclopedia/congress-racial-
equality-core

[265] How The GI Bill's Promise Was Denied To A Million Black WWII Veterans - https://www.history.com/news/gi-bill-black-wwii-veterans-benefits

[266] How African American WWII Veterans Were Scorned By The G.I. Bill - https://progressive.org/dispatches/how-african-american-wwii-veterans-were-scorned-by-the-g-i-b/

[267] After The War: Blacks And The GI Bill - https://americanexperience.si.edu/wp-content/uploads/2015/02/after-the-war-blacks-and-the-gi-bill.pdf

[268] White Flight (New Orleans Case Study) - http://www.datacenterresearch.org/pre-katrina/tertiary/white.html

[269] White Flight Alive And Well - https://www.theatlantic.com/business/archive/2015/07/white-flight-alive-and-well/399980/

[270] The Groveland Four (1949) - https://www.blackpast.org/african-american-history/the-groveland-four-1949/

[271] Four Black Men Wrongly Charged With Rape Are Exonerated 72 Years Later - https://www.nytimes.com/2021/11/22/us/groveland-four-exonerated-florida.html

[272] The Groveland Four, A Podcast - https://www.pbs.org/show/groveland-four/

[273] African Americans In The Korean War - https://koreanwarlegacy.org/chapters/african-americans-in-the-korean-war/

[274] A 'Forgotten History' Of How The U.S. Government Segregated America - https://www.npr.org/2017/05/03/526655831/a-forgotten-history-of-how-the-u-s-government-segregated-america

[275] The Racial Segregation Of American Cities Was Anything But Accidental - https://www.smithsonianmag.com/history/how-federal-government-intentionally-racially-segregated-american-cities-180963494/

[276] Richard Rothstein, The Color of Law: The Forgotten History of How Our Government Segregated America

[277] July 11, 1951: Cicero Riot Over Housing Desegregation - https://www.zinnedproject.org/news/tdih/cicero-riot

[278] Pauli Murray's Indelible Mark On The Fight For Equal Rights - https://www.aclu.org/issues/womens-rights/pauli-murrays-indelible-mark-fight-equal-rights

[279] Landmark Cases, Brown V. Board Of Education - https://www.thirteen.org/wnet/supremecourt/rights/landmark_brown.html
[280] History - Brown V. Board Of Education Re-Enactment - https://www.uscourts.gov/educational-resources/educational-activities/history-brown-v-board-education-re-enactment

[281] Black And White In Vietnam - https://www.nytimes.com/2017/07/18/opinion/racism-vietnam-war.html

[282] As Da 5 Bloods Hits Netflix, Black Vietnam Veterans Recall The Real Injustices They Faced During And After The War - https://time.com/5852476/da-5-bloods-black-vietnam-veterans/

[283] The Forgotten History Of A Prison Uprising In Vietnam - https://www.npr.org/sections/codeswitch/2018/08/29/642617106/the-forgotten-history-of-a-prison-uprising-in-vietnam

[284] Before Rosa Parks, There Was Claudette Colvin - https://www.npr.org/2009/03/15/101719889/before-rosa-parks-there-was-claudette-colvin

[285] The Murder Of Emmett Till - https://www.pbs.org/wgbh/americanexperience/features/till-timeline/

[286] The Murder Of Emmett Till, Library Of Congress - https://www.loc.gov/collections/civil-rights-history-project/articles-and-essays/murder-of-emmett-till/

[287] Emmett Till's Enduring Legacy - https://www.nytimes.com/article/who-was-emmett-till.html

[288] Rosa Parks - https://www.history.com/topics/black-history/rosa-parks

[289] Montgomery Bus Boycott - https://kinginstitute.stanford.edu/encyclopedia/montgomery-bus-boycott

[290] Rosa Parks, Martin Luther King Jr., And The Montgomery Bus Boycott - https://billofrightsinstitute.org/essays/rosa-parks-martin-luther-king-jr-and-the-montgomery-bus-boycott

[291] COINTELPRO - https://vault.fbi.gov/cointel-pro

[292] COINTELPRO And The History Of Domestic Spying - https://www.npr.org/templates/story/story.php?storyid=5161811

[293] COINTELPRO [Counterintelligence Program] (1956-1976) - https://www.blackpast.org/african-american-history/cointelpro-1956-1976/

[294] The FBI Sets Goals For COINTELPRO - https://shec.ashp.cuny.edu/items/show/814

[295] Southern Christian Leadership Council (SCLC) -
https://kinginstitute.stanford.edu/encyclopedia/southern
-christian-leadership-conference-sclc

[296] The Little Rock Nine -
https://nmaahc.si.edu/explore/stories/little-rock-nine

[297] Civil Rights Act Of 1957 - http://www.african-american-civil-rights.org/civil-rights-act-of-1957/

[298] The Civil Rights Act Of 1957 -
https://history.house.gov/historical-highlights/1951-2000/the-civil-rights-act-of-1957/

[299] Greensboro Four: David Richmond, Franklin Mccain, Ezell Blair Jr. (Jibreel Khazan), Joe Mcneil -
https://www.ncpedia.org/greensboro-four

[300] SNCC - https://www.history.com/topics/black-history/sncc

[301] John F. Kennedy, Martin Luther King Jr., and the Phone Call That Changed History - https://time.com/4817240/martin-luther-king-john-kennedy-phone-call/

[302] The Tougaloo Nine - https://www.blackpast.org/african-american-history/groups-organizations-african-american-history/the-tougaloo-nine-1961/

[303] Freedom Rides -
https://kinginstitute.stanford.edu/encyclopedia/freedom-rides#:~:text=the%20freedom%20rides%20were%20fi,segregation%20on%20interstate%20buses%20unconstitutional

[304] The Rise Of The SWAT Team In American Policing -
https://www.nytimes.com/2014/09/08/us/the-rise-of-the-swat
-team-in-american-policing.html

[305] Don't Forget That Martin Luther King Jr. Was Once Denounced as an Extremist - https://time.com/5099513/martin-luther-king-day-myths/

[306] American Rhetoric, Top 100 Speeches - https://www.americanrhetoric.com/top100speechesall.html

[307] Malcolm X at Oxford: 'They're going to kill me soon' - https://www.theguardian.com/film/2019/feb/19/malcolm-x-oxford-kill-me-soon-assassination-tariq-ali

[308] Malcolm X, "The Ballot or the Bullet," April 12, 1964 - https://billofrightsinstitute.org/activities/malcolm-x-the-ballot-or-the-bullet-april-12-1964

[309] American Rhetoric, Top 100 Speeches - https://www.americanrhetoric.com/top100speechesall.html

[310] Fannie Lou Hamer's "I Question America" Testimony - https://mississippiencyclopedia.org/entries/fannie-lou-hamer-i-question-america-testimony/

[311] 'I Question America': Remembering Fannie Lou Hamer's Challenge To White Supremacy - https://www.facingsouth.org/2014/08/i-question-america-remembering-fannie-lou-hamers-c.html

[312] Freedom Summer (History) - https://www.history.com/topics/black-history/freedom-summer

[313] Freedom Summer (King Institute) – https://kinginstitute.stanford.edu/encyclopedia/freedom-summer

[314] Murder In Mississippi - https://www.pbs.org/wgbh/americanexperience/features/freedomsummer-murder/

[315] Remembering A Civil Rights Swim-In: 'It Was A Milestone' - https://www.npr.org/2014/06/13/321380585/remembering-a-civil-rights-swim-in-it-was-a-milestone

[316] The Haunting Story Behind This Picture Of Malcolm X And Martin Luther King - https://www.indy100.com/news/photo-of-martin-luther-king-and-malcom-x-is-an-important-reminder-of-what-the-world-has-lost-anniversary-8284721

[317] Martin Luther King Jr. Met Malcolm X Just Once. The Photo Still Haunts Us With What Was Lost. - https://www.washingtonpost.com/news/retropolis/wp/2018/01/14/martin-luther-king-jr-met-malcolm-x-just-once-the-photo-still-haunts-us-with-what-was-lost/

[318] 56 Years Ago, He Shot Malcolm X. Now He Lives Quietly In Brooklyn. - https://www.nytimes.com/2021/11/22/nyregion/malcolm-x-assassination-halim-hayer.html

[319] Malcolm X Assassinated - https://www.history.com/this-day-in-history/malcolm-x-assassinated

[320] The Enduring Mystery Of Malcolm X's Assassination - https://time.com/5778688/malcolm-x-assassination/

[321] Timeline Of Malcolm X's Life - https://www.pbs.org/wgbh/americanexperience/features/malcolmx-timeline-malcolm-xs-life/

[322] Reeb, James - https://kinginstitute.stanford.edu/encyclopedia/reeb-james

[323] March 25, 1965: Viola Liuzzo Murdered by KKK After Selma to Montgomery March - https://www.zinnedproject.org/news/tdih/viola-liuzzo-murdered-by-kkk

[324] Killed For Taking Part In 'Everybody's Fight' - https://www.npr.org/sections/codeswitch/2013/08/12/2095959 35/killed-for-taking-part-in-everybody-s-fight

[325] Watts Riot - https://www.history.com/topics/1960s/watts-riots

[326] The Pioneering Pauli Murray: Lawyer, Activist, Scholar And Priest - https://nmaahc.si.edu/explore/stories/pioneering-pauli-murray-lawyer-activist-scholar-and-priest

[327] Meredith March Against Fear, June 1966 - https://exhibits.stanford.edu/fitch/browse/meredith-march-against-fear-june-1966

[328] Black Panther Party (U.S.A.) - https://www.blackpast.org/african-american-history/black-panther-party/

[329] The Black Panther Party: Challenging Police And Promoting Social Change - https://nmaahc.si.edu/explore/stories/black-panther-party-challenging-police-and-promoting-social-change

[330] The Black Panther Party - https://www.archives.gov/research/african-americans/black-power/black-panthers

[331] The Black Panther Party Ten-Point Program - https://www.blackpast.org/african-american-history/primary-documents-african-american-history/black-panther-party-ten-point-program-1966/

[332] Qualified Immunity Explained - https://theappeal.org/qualified-immunity-explained/

[333] Qualified Immunity (Law) - https://www.law.cornell.edu/wex/qualified_immunity

[334] Project 100,000: The Great Society 'S Answer To Military Manpower Needs In Vietnam - https://digitalcommons.lasalle.edu/cgi/viewcontent.cgi?referer= https://www.google.com/&httpsredir=1&article=1014&context= vietnamgeneration

[335] Project 100,000 (1966-1971) - https://www.blackpast.org/global-african-history/project-100-000-1966-1971/

[336] Thirty Years Of America's Drug War, A Chronology - https://www.pbs.org/wgbh/pages/frontline/shows/drugs/cron/index.html#8

[337] Was Nixon's War On Drugs A Racially Motivated Crusade? It's A Bit More Complicated. - https://www.vox.com/2016/3/29/11325750/nixon-war-on-drugs

[338] Poor People's Campaign - https://kinginstitute.stanford.edu/encyclopedia/poor-peoples-campaign

[339] Understanding Detroit's 1967 Upheaval 50 Years Later - https://www.smithsonianmag.com/history/understanding- detroits-1967-upheaval-50-years-later-180964212/

[340] Stokely Carmichael - https://www.history.com/topics/black-history/stokely-carmichael

[341] Carmichael, Stokely - https://kinginstitute.stanford.edu/encyclopedia/carmichael-stokely

[342] Why Martin Luther King's Family Believes James Earl Ray Was Not His Killer - https://www.history.com/news/who-killed-martin-luther-king-james-earl-ray-mlk-assassination

[343] History Of Fair Housing -
https://www.hud.gov/program_offices/fair_housing_equal_opp
/aboutfheo/history#:~:text=the%201968%20act%20expanded%20
on,housing%20act%20(of%201968)

[344] Why Black American Athletes Raised Their Fists At The 1968
Olympics - https://www.history.com/news/black-athletes-raise-
fists-1968-olympics

[345] Did You Know? KSU First To Celebrate Black History Month -
https://www.kent.edu/cas/did-you-
know#:~:text=in%20february%201970%2c%20kent%20state,which
%20was%20established%20in%201976.&text=since%201976%2c%
2
0each%20president%20has,month%20and%20endorsed%20a%20t
heme

[346] FBI Wanted Poster For Angela Davis -
https://nmaahc.si.edu/object/nmaahc_2012.60.8

[347] Biography Of Angela Davis, Political Activist And Academic -
https://www.thoughtco.com/angela-davis-biography-3528285

[348] Gladys Mae West - https://www.blackpast.org/african-
american-history/people-african-american-history/gladys-mae-
west-1930/

[349] NBC Reporter Recalls Exposing FBI Spying -
https://www.nbcnews.com/news/investigations/nbc-reporter-
recalls-exposing-fbi-spying-n5901

[350] Burglars In 1971 FBI Office Break-In Come Forward After 43
Years - https://www.theguardian.com/world/2014/jan/07/fbi-
office-break-in-1971-come-forward-documents

[351] COINTELPRO: The Untold American Story -
https://cldc.org/wp-content/uploads/2011/12/cointelpro.pdf

[352] Congressional Black Caucus (CBC) - https://www.archives.gov/research/african-americans/black-power/cbc#:~:text=the%20congressional%20black%20caucus%20(cbc,african%20american%20members%20of%20congress

[353] CBC History - https://cbc.house.gov/history/

[354] March 25, 1971, 61 Recommendations To President Nixon - https://cbc.house.gov/uploadedfiles/cbc_letter_to_nixon.pdf

[355] Fifty Years Ago Today, President Nixon Declared The War On Drugs - https://www.vera.org/blog/fifty-years-ago-today-president-nixon-declared-the-war-on-drugs

[356] A History Of The Drug War - https://Drugpolicy.Org/Issues/Brief-History-Drug-War

[357] Southern Strategy - https://www.encyclopedia.com/social-sciences/applied-and-social-sciences-magazines/southern-strategy

[358] Was Nixon's War On Drugs A Racially Motivated Crusade? It's A Bit More Complicated. - https://www.vox.com/2016/3/29/11325750/nixon-war-on-drugs

[359] MOVE (1972 - ) - https://www.blackpast.org/african-american-history/groups-organizations-african-american-history/move-1972/

[360] Kelley Apologizes For F.B.I. Actions - https://www.nytimes.com/1976/05/09/archives/kelley-apologizes-for-fbi-actions.html

[361] Sterilized By North Carolina, She Felt Raped Once More - https://www.latimes.com/archives/la-xpm-2012-jan-25-la-na-forced-sterilization-20120126-story.html

[362] N.C. Considers Paying Forced Sterilization Victims - https://www.npr.org/2011/06/22/137347548/n-c-considers-paying-forced-sterilization-victims

[363] Victims Of Forced Sterilization To Receive $10 Million From North Carolina - https://www.nbcnews.com/nightly-news/victims-forced-sterilization-receive-10-million-north-carolina-flna6c10753957

[364] The U.S. Government's Role In Sterilizing Women Of Color - https://www.thoughtco.com/u-s-governments-role-sterilizing-women-of-color-2834600

[365] Regents Of University Of California V. Bakke (1978) - https://www.thirteen.org/wnet/supremecourt/rights/landmark_regents.html#:~:text=bakke%20(1978)-,in%20regents%20of%20university%20of%20california%20v.,was%20constitutional%20in%20some%20circumstances

[366] Critical Race Theory: A Brief History - https://www.nytimes.com/article/what-is-critical-race-theory.html

[367] The True History Of America's Private Prison Industry - https://time.com/5405158/the-true-history-of-americas-private-prison-industry/

[368] Corrections Corporation Of America (Now Corecivic) - http://www.correctionscorp.com/

[369] The Day Philadelphia Bombed Its Own People - https://www.vox.com/the-highlight/2019/8/8/20747198/philadelphia-bombing-1985-move

[370] The Iran-Contra Affair - https://www.pbs.org/wgbh/americanexperience/features/reagan-iran/

[371] The Iran Contra Affair, Brown -
https://www.brown.edu/research/understanding_the_iran_cont
ra_affair/iran-contra-affairs.php

[372] The CIA, Contras, Gangs, And Crack - https://ips-
dc.org/the_cia_contras_gangs_and_crack/

[373] Cocaine, Conspiracy Theories And The CIA In Central America
-
https://www.pbs.org/wgbh/pages/frontline/shows/drugs/spe
cial/cia.html

[374] The CIA-Contra-Crack Cocaine Controversy: A Review Of The
Justice Department's Investigations And Prosecutions -
https://oig.justice.gov/sites/default/files/archive/special/9712/
ch01p1.htm

[375] Thirty Years Of America's Drug War, A Chronology -
https://www.pbs.org/wgbh/pages/frontline/shows/drugs/cro
n/index.html#8

[376] Crack-Cocaine Disparity -
https://www.aclu.org/other/cracks-system-20-years-unjust
- federal-crack-cocaine-law

[377] George H.W. Bush's "Willie Horton" Ad Will Always Be The
Reference Point For Dog-Whistle Racism -
https://www.vox.com/2018/12/1/18121221/george-hw-bush-
willie-horton-dog-whistle-politics

[378] Bush Made Willie Horton An Issue In 1988, And The Racial
Scars Are Still Fresh -
https://www.nytimes.com/2018/12/03/us/politics/bush-willie
- horton.html

[379] George Bush And Willie Horton -
https://www.nytimes.com/1988/11/04/opinion/george-bush-
and-willie-horton.html

[380] Racial Stereotypes And White's Political Views Of Blacks In The Context Of Welfare And Crime - https://www.researchgate.net/publication/270179277_racial_ster eotypes_and_whites'_political_views_of_blacks_in_the_context_of _welfare_and_crime

[381] Fair Sentencing Act - https://www.aclu.org/issues/criminal-law-reform/drug-law-reform/fair-sentencing-act#:~:text=the%20scientifically%20unjustifiable%20100%3a1,form s%20of%20the%20same%20drug

[382] War In The Gulf: The Troops; Blacks Wary Of Their Big Role As Troops - https://www.nytimes.com/1991/01/25/us/war-in-the-gulf-the-troops-blacks-wary-of-their-big-role-as-troops.html

[383] LAPD Officers Beat Rodney King On Camera - https://www.history.com/this-day-in-history/police-brutality-caught-on-video

[384] The Long Crusade Of Clarence And Ginni Thomas - https://www.nytimes.com/2022/02/22/magazine/clarence-thomas-ginni-thomas.html

[385] Where Is Soon Ja Du Now? She Fatally Shot Latasha Harlins in 1991 - https://www.distractify.com/p/soon-ja-du-now

[386] When LA Erupted In Anger: A Look Back At The Rodney King Riots - https://www.npr.org/2017/04/26/524744989/when-la-erupted-in-anger-a-look-back-at-the-rodney-king-riots

[387] Riots Erupt In Los Angeles After Police Officers Are Acquitted In Rodney King Trial - https://www.history.com/this-day-in-history/riots-erupt-in-los-angeles

[388] 1033 Program - https://www.wired.com/story/pentagon-hand-me-downs-militarize-police-1033-program/

[389] How America's Police Became An Army: The 1033 Program - https://www.newsweek.com/how-americas-police-became-army-1033-program-264537

[390] Three Strikes Basics - https://law.stanford.edu/three-strikes-project/three-strikes-basics/#:~:text=in%201994%2c%20california%20voters%20enacte d,kimber%20reynolds%20and%20polly%20klaas

[391] Did The 1994 Crime Bill Cause Mass Incarceration? - https://www.brookings.edu/blog/fixgov/2020/08/28/did-the-1994-crime-bill-cause-mass-incarceration/

[392] 3 Ways The 1994 Crime Bill Continues To Hurt Communities Of Color - https://www.americanprogress.org/issues/race/news/2019/05/10/469642/3-ways-1994-crime-bill-continues-hurt-communities-color/#:~:text=2.,two%20convictions%20on%20their%20record

[393] The Controversial 1994 Crime Law That Joe Biden Helped Write, Explained - https://www.vox.com/policy-and-politics/2019/6/20/18677998/joe-biden-1994-crime-bill-law-mass-incarceration

[394] The Clinton-Backed 1994 Crime Law Had Many Flaws. But It Didn't Create Mass Incarceration - https://www.vox.com/2016/2/11/10961362/clinton-1994-crime-law

[395] Mass Incarceration Is About Way More Than The War On Drugs - https://www.vox.com/2015/7/16/8978579/war-on-drugs-mass-incarceration

[396] Legalize It All: How To Win The War On Drugs By Dan Baum - https://harpers.org/archive/2016/04/legalize-it-all/

[397] Thirty Years Of America's Drug War, A Chronology - https://www.pbs.org/wgbh/pages/frontline/shows/drugs/cro n/index.html#8

[398] Stokely Carmichael, Rights Leader Who Coined 'Black Power,' Dies At 57 - https://www.nytimes.com/1998/11/16/us/stokely-carmichael-rights-leader-who-coined-black-power-dies-at-57.html

[399] Racial Segregation In The 2000 Census: Promising News - https://www.brookings.edu/wp-content/uploads/2016/06/glaeser.pdf

[400] The Global War On Terrorism: The First 100 Days - https://2001-2009.state.gov/s/ct/rls/wh/6947.htm

[401] Black Ops: Black Masculinity And The War On Terror - https://www.jstor.org/stable/43823396

[402] Thomas Blanton, Who Bombed a Birmingham Church, Dies at 82 - https://www.nytimes.com/2020/06/26/us/thomas-blanton-dead.html

[403] White Flight, A New Orleans Case Study - https://www.datacenterresearch.org/pre-katrina/tertiary/white.html

[404] Race, Socioeconomic Status, And Return Migration To New Orleans After Hurricane Katrina - https://www.ncbi.nlm.nih.gov/pmc/articles/pmc2862006/

[405] White New Orleans Has Recovered, Black New Orleans Has Not - https://talkpoverty.org/2016/08/29/white-new-orleans-recovered-hurricane-katrina-black-new-orleans-not/

[406] Katrina Washed Away New Orleans's Black Middle Class - https://fivethirtyeight.com/features/katrina-washed-away-new-orleanss-black-middle-class/

[407] 7 Ways The Obama Administration Has Accelerated Police Militarization - https://www.huffpost.com/entry/obama-police-militarization_n_3566478

[408] The Pentagon's Hand-Me-Downs Helped Militarize Police. Here's How - https://www.wired.com/story/pentagon-hand-me-downs-militarize-police-1033-program/

[409] The 2008 Crash: What Happened to All That Money? - https://www.history.com/news/2008-financial-crisis-causes

[410] The 2007–2008 Financial Crisis in Review - https://www.investopedia.com/articles/economics/09/financial-crisis-review.asp

[411] The Stock Market Crash Of 2008 - https://www.thebalance.com/stock-market-crash-of-2008-3305535

[412] 2008-2009 Wall Street Crash (History) - https://www.history.com/news/2008-financial-crisis-causes

[413] Blacks Not Recovered From 2008-2009 Wall Street Crash - https://www.marketwatch.com/story/these-numbers-prove-african-americans-still-havent-recovered-from-the-financial-crisis-2019-02-06

[414] Black Median Income To ZERO By 2053 - https://ips-dc.org/report-the-road-to-zero-wealth/

[415] Recession Racial Slant - https://www.theatlantic.com/business/archive/2015/06/black-recession-housing-race/396725/

[416] What to know about Ketanji Brown Jackson, Biden's pick for the Supreme Court - https://www.washingtonpost.com/politics/2022/02/25/what-know-about-ketanji-brown-jackson-bidens-pick-supreme-court/

[417] For African Americans, 50 Years Of High Unemployment - https://www.epi.org/publication/african-americans-50-years-high-unemployment/

[418] Unemployment 1974-2020 (FRED Economic Research) - https://fred.stlouisfed.org/series/lns14000031

[419] Unemployment Black Unemployment Rate Is Consistently Twice That Of Whites - https://www.pewresearch.org/fact-tank/2013/08/21/through-good-times-and-bad-black-unemployment-is-consistently-double-that-of-whites/

[420] 'Race And The Obama Administration' Explores Substance, Symbols And Promises Kept - https://news.emory.edu/stories/2019/07/er_gillespie_obama_administration/campus.html

[421] Fair Sentencing Act - https://www.aclu.org/issues/criminal-law-reform/drug-law-reform/fair-sentencing-act

[422] Kids For Cash - https://www.npr.org/sections/thetwo-way/2011/08/11/139536686/pa-judge-sentenced-to-28-years-in-massive-juvenile-justice-bribery-scandal#:~:text=live%20sessions-,judge%20sentenced%20to%2028%20years%20in%20bribery%20scandal%20%3a%20the%20two,4%2c000%20convictions%20issued%20by%20ciavarella.

[423] Wells Fargo "Ghetto Loans" - https://www.pbs.org/wnet/need-to-know/opinion/wells-fargo-settlement-an-important-victory-for-minority-homeowners-communities/14150/

[424] The Race Gap. Black, White: Retirement - https://graphics.reuters.com/global-race/usa/nmopajawjva/#retirement

[425] The BLM Movement - https://www.blackpast.org/black-lives-matter-movement-2013/

[426] BLM vs ALM (Pew) -
https://www.pewresearch.org/internet/2016/08/15/the-hashtag-blacklivesmatter-emerges-social-activism-on-twitter
/

[427] Progress Of The African-American Community During The Obama Administration -
https://obamawhitehouse.archives.gov/the-press-office/2016/10/14/progress-african-american-community-during-obama-administration

[428] 2012 Report To The Congress: Continuing Impact Of United States V. Booker On Federal Sentencing -
https://www.ussc.gov/research/congressional-reports/2012-report-congress-continuing-impact-united-states-v-booker-federal-sentencing

[429] Was Nixon's War On Drugs A Racially Motivated Crusade? It's A Bit More Complicated. -
https://www.vox.com/2016/3/29/11325750/nixon-war-on-drugs

[430] Black Lives Matter: Eliminating Racial Inequity In The Criminal Justice System - https://www.sentencingproject.org/wp-content/uploads/2015/11/black-lives-matter.pdf

[431] School Segregation (Ferguson Study) -
https://www.propublica.org/article/ferguson-school-segregation

[432] Civil Rights Data Collection On Equity And Opportunity Gaps In Schools -
https://www2.ed.gov/about/offices/list/ocr/docs/2013-14-first-look.pdf

[433] Apartheid Schools -
https://www.theatlantic.com/politics/archive/2015/07/even-after-neighborhoods-integrate-many-students-attend-apartheid-schools/432435/

[434] Pew Research Center, Personal Experiences With Discrimination - https://www.pewresearch.org/social-trends/2016/06/27/5-personal-experiences-with-discrimination/

[435] On Views Of Race And Inequality, Blacks And Whites Are Worlds Apart - https://wispd.org/attachments/article/254/st_2016.06.27_race-inequality-final.pdf

[436] Donald Trump Is The Accelerant - https://www.vox.com/21506029/trump-violence-tweets-racist- hate-speech

[437] White Extremism Under Trump Rises 55% - https://www.aa.com.tr/en/americas/white-extremism-under-trump-presidency-rises-55-study/1772045

[438] The Rise Of White Nationalism - https://cnsmaryland.org/2020/04/02/with-rise-of-trump-came-rise-of-white-nationalism-critics-say/

[439] White Supremacy And Trump - https://www.npr.org/2019/06/23/735191317/white-supremacy-and-trump

[440] No, Trump Hasn't Been The Best President For Black America Since Lincoln - https://www.vox.com/21524499/what-trump-has-done-for-black-people

[441] Has Trump Failed Black Americans? - https://www.brookings.edu/blog/how-we-rise/2020/10/15/has-trump-failed-black-americans/amp/

[442] Woman Linked To 1955 Emmett Till Murder Tells Historian Her Claims Were False - https://www.nytimes.com/2017/01/27/us/emmett-till-lynching-carolyn-bryant-donham.html

[443] The Race Gap. Black, White: Pregnancy-Related Deaths - https://graphics.reuters.com/global-race/usa/nmopajawjva/#food-insecurity

[444] The Race Gap. Black, White: Educational Attainment - https://graphics.reuters.com/global-race/usa/nmopajawjva/#educational-attainment

[445] The Race Gap. Black, White: The Justice System - https://graphics.reuters.com/global-race/usa/nmopajawjva/#the-justice-system

[446] The 100 Best Bostonians Of All Time - https://www.bostonmagazine.com/news/2016/01/05/100-best-bostonians/
[447] Uncle Nearest Premium Whiskey - https://unclenearest.com/
[448] Unrest In Virginia - https://time.com/charlottesville-white-nationalist-rally-clashes/

[449] In Context: Donald Trump's 'Very Fine People On Both Sides' Remarks (Transcript) - https://www.politifact.com/article/2019/apr/26/context-trumps-very-fine-people-both-sides-remarks/

[450] The Race Gap. Black, White: The Justice System - https://graphics.reuters.com/global-race/usa/nmopajawjva/#the-justice-system

[451] How Unlikely Allies Got Prison Reform Done—With An Assist From Kim Kardashian West - https://time.com/5486560/prison-reform-jared-kushner-kim-kardashian-west/

[452] The First Step Act, Explained - https://www.vox.com/future-perfect/2018/12/18/18140973/state-of-the-union-trump-first-step-act-criminal-justice-reform

[453] Federal Bureau Of Prisons - An Overview Of The First Step Act - https://www.bop.gov/inmates/fsa/overview.jsp

[454] The Race Gap. Black, White: Food Insecurity - https://graphics.reuters.com/global-race/usa/nmopajawjva/#food-insecurity

[455] Frustration And Fury As Rand Paul Holds Up Anti-Lynching Bill In Senate - https://www.nytimes.com/2020/06/05/us/politics/rand-paul-anti-lynching-bill-senate.html

[456] Trump: Black Lives Matter Is A 'Symbol Of Hate' - https://www.politico.com/news/2020/07/01/trump-black-lives-matter-347051

[457] Lootin' To Shootin' - https://www.npr.org/2020/05/29/864818368/the-history-behind-when-the-looting-starts-the-shooting-starts

[458] Correcting Past Mistakes: PPP Loans and Black-Owned Small Businesses - https://www.acslaw.org/expertforum/correcting-past-mistakes-ppp-loans-and-black-owned-small-businesses/

[459] Automation in Small Business Lending Can Reduce Racial Disparities: Evidence from the Paycheck Protection Program - https://papers.ssrn.com/sol3/papers.cfm?abstract_id=3939384

[460] The Paycheck Protection Program failed many Black-owned businesses - https://www.vox.com/2020/10/5/21427881/paycheck-protection-program-black-owned-businesses

[461] Minority Entrepreneurs Struggled to Get Small-Business Relief Loans - https://www.nytimes.com/2021/04/04/business/ppp-loans-minority-businesses.html

[462] Building on a Month of Strong Results, Biden-Harris Administration Takes Steps to Further Promote Relief for

America's Black-Owned Businesses –
https://www.sba.gov/sites/default/files/2021
- 02/2021.02.22%20-
%20sba%20ppp%20reforms%20and%20actions%20fact%20sheet%
20-%20black%20communities%20summary-508.pdf

[463] Redlining Still Affecting Blacks Today -
https://www.washingtonpost.com/news/wonk/wp/2018/03/
2
8/redlining-was-banned-50-years-ago-its-still-hurting-minorities-
today/

[464] Why Racism In Health Care Is Still A Problem Today -
https://www.thoughtco.com/racism-in-health-care-still-a-
problem-2834530

[465] Coronavirus In African Americans And Other People Of Color
- https://www.hopkinsmedicine.org/health/conditions-and-
diseases/coronavirus/covid19-racial-disparities

[466] The Color Of Coronavirus: Covid-19 Deaths By Race And
Ethnicity In The U.S. -
https://www.apmresearchlab.org/covid/deaths-by-race

[467] A Penny On The Dollar Study -
https://journals.sagepub.com/doi/full/10.1177/2378023120916
6 16

[468] Quaker Oats To Retire Aunt Jemima After Acknowledging
Brand's Origins As 'Racial Stereotype' -
https://www.smithsonianmag.com/smart-news/quaker-oats
- will-retire-aunt-jemima-logo-180975127/

[469] Uncle Ben's Changing Name To Ben's Original After Criticism
Of Racial Stereotyping - https://www.npr.org/sections/live-
updates-protests-for-racial-justice/2020/09/23/916012582/uncle-
bens-changing-name-to-ben-s-original-after-criticism-of-racial-
stereotyping

[470] Appeals Court Upholds Texas Governor's Restriction On Mail-In Ballot Drop Boxes - https://www.theguardian.com/us-news/2020/oct/13/texas-mail-in-ballot-drop-box-appeals-court

[471] How Black Americans Saved Biden And American Democracy - https://www.brookings.edu/blog/how-we-rise/2020/11/24/how-black-americans-saved-biden-and-american-democracy/amp/

[472] Report Cites New Details Of Trump Pressure On Justice Dept. Over Election - https://www.nytimes.com/2021/10/06/us/politics/trump-election-fraud-report.html

[473] Trump's Mixed Message: Stop The Count Or Keep Counting? - https://www.latimes.com/politics/story/2020-11-05/trumps-mixed-message-stop-the-count-or-keep-counting

[474] Trump's Desperate "STOP THE COUNT!" Tweet, Briefly Explained - https://www.vox.com/2020/11/5/21550880/trump-tweet-stop-the-count-votes-presidential-election

[475] Wife Of Justice Thomas Rebuts Claims Of Conflict Of Interest - https://www.npr.org/2022/03/14/1086535100/wife-of-justice-thomas-rebuts-claims-of-conflict-of-interest

[476] Capitol Riot Investigations - https://www.nytimes.com/spotlight/us-capitol-riots - investigations

[477] A Look Back At Americans' Reactions To The Jan. 6 Riot At The U.S. Capitol - https://www.pewresearch.org/fact-tank/2022/01/04/a-look-back-at-americans-reactions-to-the-jan-6-riot-at-the-u-s-capitol/

[478] Nooses spotted as pro-Trump rioters spark chaos and lawlessness on Capitol Hill -

https://www.businessinsider.com/nooses-spotted-as-pro-trump-rioters-spark-chaos-on-capitol-2021-1

[479] These Are The First Military Bases Whose Confederate Names Could Be Changed - https://www.military.com/daily-news/2021/05/21/these-are-first-military-bases-whose-confederate-names-could-be-changed.html

[480] How Texas Plans To Make Its House Districts Even Redder - https://www.nytimes.com/interactive/2021/10/03/us/politics/texas-redistricting-map-2022.html

[481] Texas Reduces Black And Hispanic Majority Congressional Districts In Proposed Map, Despite People Of Color Fueling Population Growth - https://www.texastribune.org/2021/09/24/texas-congressional-redistricting/

[482] Explaining The Impact Of Redistricting In Texas, Visually - https://www.nytimes.com/2021/10/18/insider/texas-redistricting.html

[483] How Maps Reshape American Politics - https://www.nytimes.com/interactive/2021/11/07/us/politics/redistricting-maps-explained.html

[484] Student Loans, The Racial Wealth Divide, And Why We Need Full Student Debt Cancellation - https://www.brookings.edu/research/student-loans-the-racial-wealth-divide-and-why-we-need-full-student-debt-cancellation/

[485] Black Farmers Fear Foreclosure As Debt Relief Remains Frozen - https://www.nytimes.com/2022/02/21/us/politics/black-farmers-debt-relief.html

[486] Black Farmers May Finally Get The Help They Deserve - https://www.nytimes.com/2021/03/04/opinion/black-farmers-covid-relief.html

THE BLACK LIST: 1526 - 2022

[487] Black neighborhood home appraisal gap is real and persistent, Freddie Mac reports - https://www.bankrate.com/mortgages/homes-in-black-neighborhoods-more-likely-to-get-low-appraisals/

[488] What Is Critical Race Theory, and Why Is It Under Attack? - https://www.edweek.org/leadership/what-is-critical-race-theory-and-why-is-it-under-attack/2021/05

[489] Governor Desantis Announces Legislative Proposal To Stop W.O.K.E. Activism And Critical Race Theory In Schools And Corporations - https://www.flgov.com/2021/12/15/governor-desantis-announces-legislative-proposal-to-stop-w-o-k-e-activism-and-critical-race-theory-in-schools-and-corporations/

[490] Why are States Banning Critical Race Theory - https://www.brookings.edu/blog/fixgov/2021/07/02/why-are-states-banning-critical-race-theory/

[491] A Black Woman On The High Court Is A Good Start. But Representation Has Limits - https://www.npr.org/2022/02/09/1078933311/black-woman-supreme-court-justice

[492] Black Voters Mull Biden's Record In Office - https://www.voanews.com/amp/black-voters-mull-biden-s-record-in-office/6365828.html

[493] Blacktrack – November 2021 - https://hitstrat.com/blacktrack-november-2021/

[494] Juneteenth Is Now A National Holiday. How Did It Come To Pass? - https://www.pbs.org/newshour/politics/juneteenth-is-now-a-national-holiday-how-did-it-come-to-pass

[495] Jackson had long been at the top of Biden's short list. - https://www.nytimes.com/2022/02/25/us/politics/biden-supreme-court-ketanji-jackson.html

[496] President Biden Nominates Ketanji Brown Jackson to Serve on the U.S. Supreme Court - https://www.whitehouse.gov/kbj/

[497] Senate Passes Anti-Lynching Bill And Sends Federal Hate Crime Legislation To Biden - https://www.npr.org/2022/03/08/1085094040/senate-passes-anti-lynching-bill-and-sends-federal-hate-crimes-legislation-to-bi

[498] H.R.55 - Emmett Till Antilynching Act - https://www.congress.gov/bill/117th-congress/house-bill/55

[499] Senate Votes 53-47 to Confirm Ketanji Brown Jackson to Supreme Court (Video Moment) - https://www.c-span.org/video/?c5010178/senate-votes-53-47-confirm-ketanji-brown-jackson-supreme-court

[500] Roll Call Vote 117th Congress - 1st Session (Yays and Nays) - https://www.senate.gov/legislative/lis/roll_call_votes/vote1171/vote_117_1_00231.htm